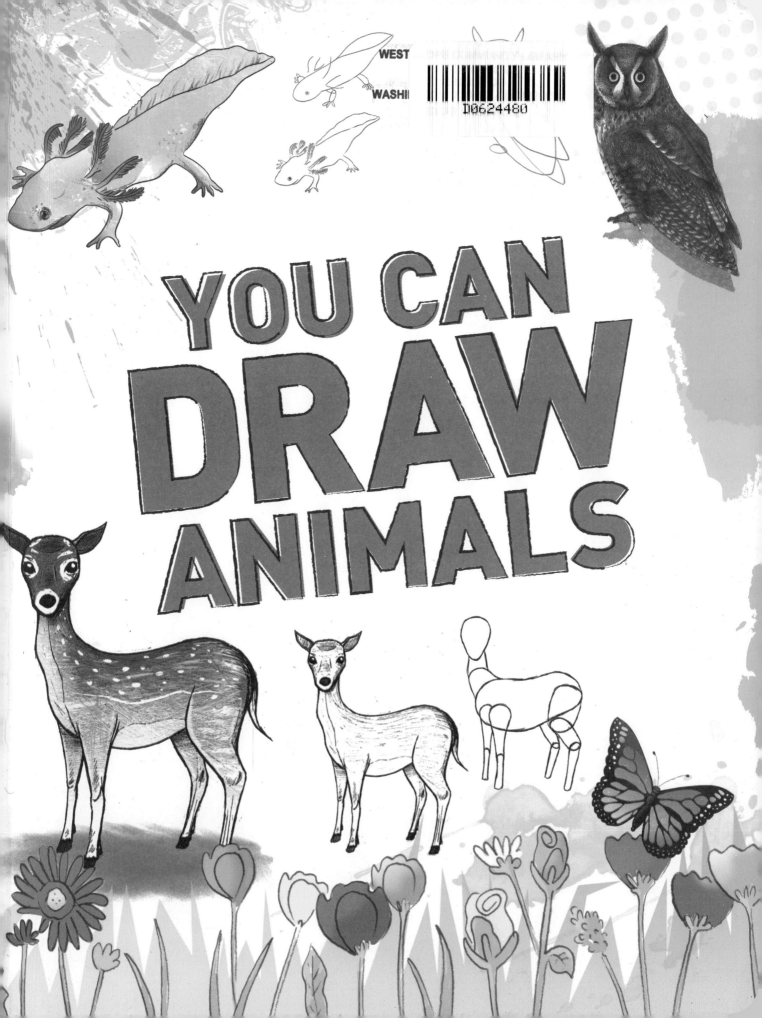

YOU CAN DRAW ANIMALS

GRAB A PENCIL AND MAKE YOUR MARK!

Flick through the pages of this book to find the animals you want to draw, then follow the steps to transform simple shapes into all kinds of creatures.

But don't just stop there! Be inspired to draw all the wildlife you see, using the tips and techniques you pick up along the way.

And remember, the more you practice, the more your confidence will grow, and the more you'll be ready to draw any animal in the world!

This edition published by Parragon Books Ltd in 2014 and distributed by

Parragon Inc.
440 Park Avenue South, 13th Floor
New York, NY 10016
www.parragon.com

Copyright © Parragon Books Ltd 2014

Illustrated by Sophie Burrows, Si Clark, Adam Fisher, Steve Horrocks, Jessica Knight, Ava Muse, Jun-gu Noh, Steve Stone
Photographs from Shutterstock, Inc.
Edited by Grace Harvey
Designed by Kathryn Davies
Production by Jonathan Wakeham

ISBN 978-1-4723-6733-4

Printed in China

Discovery KIDS™

YOU CAN DRAW ANIMALS

PaRragon

Bath · New York · Cologne · Melbourne · Delhi
Hong Kong · Shenzhen · Singapore · Amsterdam

CONTENTS

MATERIALS

ALL YOU REALLY NEED TO DRAW IS A PENCIL AND SOME PAPER, BUT OTHER MATERIALS CAN HELP TRANSFORM YOUR WORK INTO A MASTERPIECE!

PAPER AND PENCILS

Different kinds of paper and pencils can dramatically alter the appearance of your drawing.

Copy paper is smooth and great for sharp pencil lines; cartridge paper is thicker and more textured, giving a softer effect; and watercolor paper keeps the color of ink and watercolor paints vibrant. Use transparent paper (trace) to copy images.

Pencils come in numbered degrees of hard and soft. For thin, fine lines, choose an H (hard) pencil, or an HB (medium) pencil. For shading and blending, use a B (soft) pencil.

ERASER

Rub away mistakes or unwanted guidelines with an eraser. Also use it to create highlights by sweeping it across your drawing.

PEN AND INK

For line art, to go over outlines, or to make objects stand out from their backgrounds, try a cartridge pen, dip pen and ink, or even a fine-tipped brush and ink.

WATERCOLOR AND COLORED PENCILS

Regular colored pencils are great for creating animal fur and feathery textures. Watercolor pencils work like regular colored pencils, but can be blended together with a wet brush to create different colors and shades.

PAINTS

For a soft, translucent effect, try watercolor, and for a heavier, more opaque finish, try gouache. For a thick, vibrant appearance and smooth, solid areas of color, try acrylic or opaque paint. You can also create these painting techniques digitally.

BRUSHES

Experiment with round brushes for washes and general painting, pointed brushes for fine detail, and flat brushes to sweep an even amount of color on bigger areas.

CRAYONS AND PENS

Crayons are great for adding texture to your picture ...

... and felt-tip pens make objects pop from their backgrounds. You can also use marker pens to outline your work and draw attention to individual elements of your drawing.

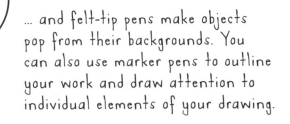

TECHNIQUES

EXPERIMENT WITH DIFFERENT DRAWING TECHNIQUES TO FIND THE RIGHT APPROACH FOR YOU!

SHAPES AND SYMMETRY
Break animals down into basic shapes and lines to help get the proportions right from the start. Then use these as a guide to create the animal's outline.

Add a center guideline for symmetrical animals, and mirror what you draw on each side.

DEPTH AND DISTANCE
Make your animals appear more realistic by including a setting in your picture. Use perspective to provide a clear foreground and background. Objects in the foreground are bigger and normally brighter.

Shadows suggest depth and distance. The higher the light source, the shorter the shadow. Use a light source and vanishing point for accurate shadows.

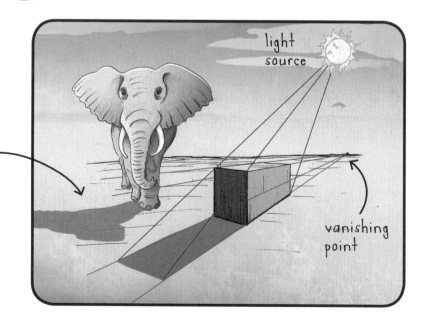

light source

vanishing point

SHADING
To give an impression of light, start with darker shades first and leave the lighter areas white. Build up the shading gradually.

For crosshatching, use the tip of the pencil to draw small lines in opposite directions.

For sketch shading, rub the side of the pencil tip on paper using varied pressure.

BRUSHSTROKES AND COLOR
There are different techniques to use when coloring. Long, sweeping brushstrokes will create a smooth appearance, while a quick jab of the brush (or stippling) adds texture.

ACTION AND MOTION
Movement can bring your animals to life. Angle hair and feathers for action poses, and create motion lines or smudgy paint marks on fast-moving animals.

ANTEATER

1

DRAW A LARGE OVAL BODY, AN OVAL TAIL, AND A CIRCLE HEAD. ADD GUIDELINES AND OVALS FOR BASIC LEGS. DRAW A CROSS IN THE BODY TO HELP POSITION THE ELONGATED SNOUT.

2

USING THE BASIC SHAPES AS A GUIDE, PENCIL IN A FLUID OUTLINE FOR YOUR GIANT ANTEATER. WORK UP THE LEGS, FEET, AND SNOUT. ADD EARS AND A DOT FOR THE EYE.

3

REFINE THE SHAPE BY ADDING FUR MARKINGS. SKETCH LINES FOR THE LONG TAIL HAIR. ADD TOES AND CLAWS TO THE FEET. WORK UP THE EYE, EARS, NOSE, AND TONGUE.

4

COLOR WITH LIGHT BROWN PAINT, BUILDING UP FUR SHADING AND TEXTURES WITH BLACK. ADD BLACK MARKINGS ACROSS THE SHOULDERS AND FEET. THEN COLOR THE TONGUE PINK.

Giant anteaters use their long saliva-covered tongues to eat— ants and termites get stuck to the sticky goo!

OWL

BARRED OWL

1

DRAW A CIRCLE AS A GUIDE FOR THE HEAD, TWO OVALS FOR THE BODY AND TAIL, AND TWO CIRCLES FOR THE FEET. ADD AN APPLE SHAPE WITHIN THE HEAD FOR THE FACE.

2

USING THE GUIDE SHAPES, SKETCH THE OWL'S OUTLINE AND ERASE UNNECESSARY LINES. ADD TWO CURVED LINES FOR THE WINGS. THEN ADD THE EYES AND A DIAMOND-SHAPED BEAK. SEPARATE THE FEET INTO TOES.

3

USE CROSSHATCHING TO SHADE IN THE FEATHERS. ADD DETAIL TO THE FACE, MAKING SURE YOU KEEP IT SYMMETRICAL. THEN COLOR WITH GRAYS AND BROWNS.

LONGEARED OWL

Start with guide shapes (for the head, body, wing, tail, and feet) to help create an outline. Then add ear, eye, and beak shapes. Color with oranges and browns, and yellow for the eyes.

BARN OWL

Draw a circle for the head and pointed ovals for the body and wing. Add a face, tail, leg, and foot, then pencil in the eyes and beak. Color with browns and grays, and yellow for the feet.

SEA OTTER

1 BEGIN BY DRAWING A LARGE SQUASHED OVAL FOR EACH OTTER'S BODY. ADD A SMALL CIRCLE FOR EACH HEAD AND SMALLER SAUSAGE SHAPES FOR THE ARMS, LEGS, AND TAIL.

2 NEXT, GO AROUND THE SHAPES WITH A SOFT PENCIL TO FIRM UP THE OVERALL OUTLINE. MAKE SURE THAT ONE OF EACH OTTER'S ARMS IS INTERLOCKING WITH THE OTHER'S.

3 ADD DOTS AND WHISKERS TO EACH OTTER'S CHEEKS, TWO EYES TO EACH FACE, DIAMOND-SHAPED NOSES, AND A LINE FOR EACH CLAW.

4 NOW IT'S TIME TO COLOR! USE BROWN AND YELLOW PENCILS TO ADD LINES AND SHADING FOR THE FUR. DRAW A FEW V SHAPES TO SHOW THE FUR IS SPIKY WHEN WET!

Sea otters often hold hands in groups while they eat, sleep, and rest, to keep family members from drifting away!

JACKrABBIT

ADULT JACKRABBITS CAN LEAP 10 FT AT A TIME, AT SPEEDS OF 35 MPH. DRAW YOURS AT FULL SPEED!

1

BEGIN BY DRAWING A CIRCLE FOR THE RABBIT'S HEAD AND THEN A LONG TAIL SHAPE TO SHOW THE SPINE.

2

ADD SQUASHED OVALS AND SAUSAGE SHAPES FOR THE LEGS. POSITION THE LEGS IN A RUNNING POSE.

3

USING A SOFT PENCIL, JOIN UP AND SMOOTH OUT THE BASIC SHAPES TO CREATE THE BODY. ADD A SNOUT TO THE HEAD.

4

ADD MORE DETAIL WITH A SHARP PENCIL.
DEFINE THE RABBIT'S NOSE, MOUTH, EARS,
EYE, TAIL, AND WHISKERS.

Once you're happy with
your jackrabbit, try
different poses!

5

USE A BROWN COLORED PENCIL OR PAINT
IN SMOOTH STROKES FOR THE FUR. SHADE
IN THE DARKER PARTS OF ITS BODY.

TARANTULA

GRAB THE BIGGEST PIECE OF PAPER YOU CAN FIND FOR THIS MEXICAN REDKNEE TARANTULA— AN ADULT FEMALE HAS A LEG SPAN OF 6 IN!

1

TO BEGIN, DRAW TWO CIRCLES FOR THE BODY—ONE FOR THE PROSOMA AND ONE FOR THE ABDOMEN. ADD EIGHT LEGS AND TWO SAUSAGE SHAPES FOR THE PINCERS.

2

USING THE GUIDE SHAPES, DRAW THE OUTLINE FOR THE TARANTULA. ADD TWO MOUTHPARTS BETWEEN THE PINCERS, STRIPES ON THE LEGS AND A PATCH ON THE BODY.

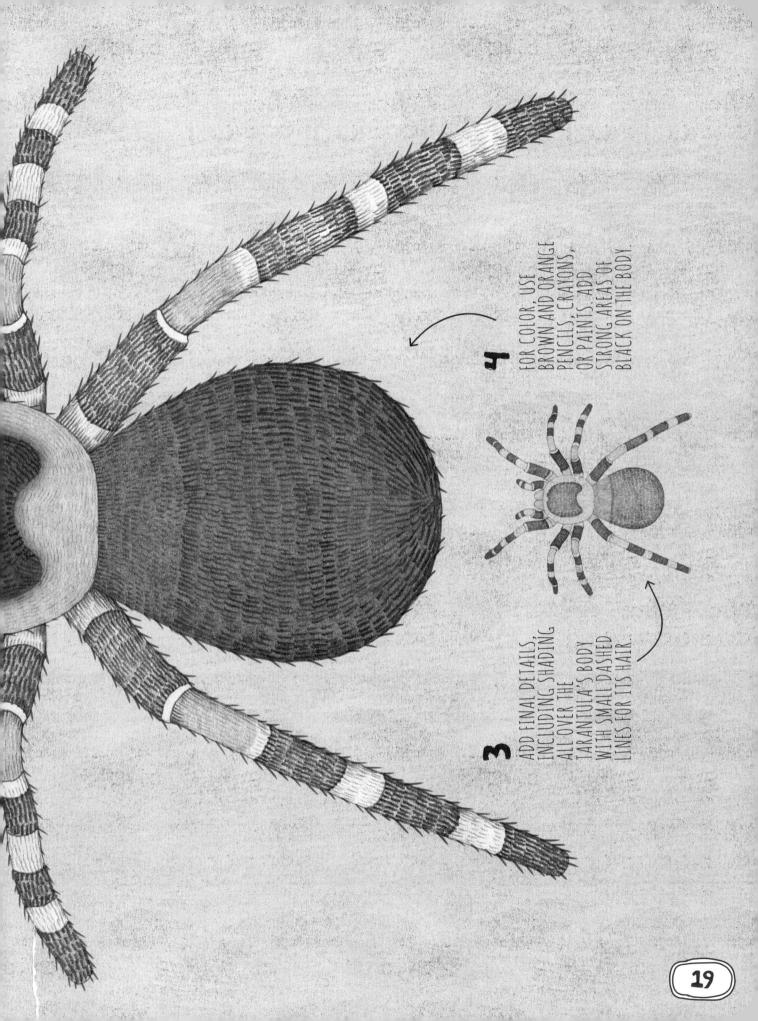

4

FOR COLOR, USE BROWN AND ORANGE PENCILS, CRAYONS, OR PAINTS. ADD STRONG AREAS OF BLACK ON THE BODY.

3

ADD FINAL DETAILS, INCLUDING SHADING, ALL OVER THE TARANTULA'S BODY WITH SMALL DASHED LINES FOR ITS HAIR.

GREEN IGUANA

1

START WITH A BASELINE FOR THE BRANCH. SKETCH A SQUASHED OVAL FOR THE IGUANA'S HEAD. ADD A LINE FOR THE BODY AND TAIL, AND LINES FOR LEGS.

2

USE A SOFT PENCIL TO GO AROUND THE SHAPES AND DRAW THE OVERALL OUTLINE. ADD SMALL HANDS, FINGERS, TWO EYELIDS, AND AN EYE.

If caught by a predator, iguanas can shed their tails to escape and regenerate a new one!

3

DRAW A ROUGH LINE DOWN THE SPINE TO USE AS A GUIDE FOR THE SPIKED RIDGE. ADD A CREST ON THE HEAD, A MOUTH LINE, AND A NOSTRIL.

4

ADD MORE DETAIL TO YOUR DRAWING, INCLUDING INDIVIDUAL SCALES, SKIN TEXTURE, CLAWS, AND LOTS OF SMALL SPIKES ON ITS BACK.

The green iguana is the largest species in the iguana family. They can be around 6 ft long from head to tail!

5

USE A GREEN WASH BASE, THEN GO OVER IT WITH GREEN FELT-TIP PENS. USE GREEN AND BROWN CRAYONS TO ADD SCALES. USE A YELLOW CRAYON FOR THE EYE.

BADGER

1

DRAW AN OVAL AS A GUIDE FOR THE HEAD, SMALL CIRCLES FOR THE NOSE AND EYES, AND WING SHAPES FOR THE EYE PATCHES AND EARS. ADD THE FRONT LEGS, THEN THE BACK LEGS AND TAIL.

2

USING THE GUIDE SHAPES, SKETCH THE OUTLINE OF THE BADGER. BREAK UP THE LINE ALL AROUND TO SHOW OFF THE FUR, THEN ADD SOME GRASS BENEATH THE FEET.

1

START WITH A BASELINE FOR THE LOG. DRAW TWO OVALS FOR THE HEAD AND MUZZLE, TWO WING SHAPES FOR THE EYE PATCHES AND EARS, AND A SEMICIRCLE FOR THE NOSE. ADD TWO LINES FOR THE SHOULDERS, TWO SMALL PAWS, AND CLAW LINES.

2

USING THE GUIDE SHAPES, DRAW THE OUTLINE OF THE BADGER. USE SMALL DASHES AROUND THE CHEEKS FOR THE FUR. ADD EYES AND EYEBROWS. SEPARATE THE PAWS INTO CLAWS.

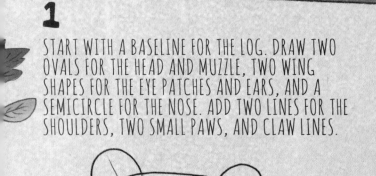

3

WITH A SOFT PENCIL, ADD SHORT FLICKS TO THE FUR, THEN SHADE IN THE EYE PATCHES AND PAWS. USE A HARDER PENCIL TO FURTHER DEFINE THE EYES, EARS, NOSE, AND MOUTH.

Varying the direction of the fur strokes will give your badger more of a 3D appearance!

3

WITH A SOFT PENCIL, ADD SHORT FLICKS FOR THE FUR, THEN SHADE IN THE EYE PATCHES AND PAWS.

A badger's claws are strong, elongated, and have a blunt end, which helps with digging.

BALD EAGLE

1 SKETCH AN OVAL BODY WITH A SMALL ROUND HEAD AND HOOKED BEAK. ADD TWO LARGER OVALS FOR THE WINGS AND A FIVE-SIDED SHAPE FOR THE TAIL.

Bald eagles are not actually bald. Their name originates from an older meaning of the words "white-headed!"

2 WITH A SOFT PENCIL, ADD A ROUGH FEATHERY OUTLINE ALL AROUND THE SHAPES, ESPECIALLY AROUND THE WINGS, TAIL, AND NECK.

3 NOW FILL IN THE BODY WITH PLENTY OF FEATHERS. USE SHORT CIRCULAR ONES FOR THE MAIN BODY AND LONGER ONES FOR THE WINGS. ADD A DOT EYE.

4 USE A SHARP PENCIL TO FURTHER DEFINE THE EAGLE. SHADE DARK AREAS UNDER THE NECK AND AROUND THE WINGS. ADD SOFT STROKES TO SHOW ITS HEAD FEATHERS.

5 PAINT THE WINGS BROWN, GRAY, AND BLACK. ADD A TOUCH OF WHITE TO THE FACE, WITH GRAY HIGHLIGHTS. USE YELLOW AND ORANGE FOR THE BEAK AND TALONS.

HUMPBACK WHALE

1

START WITH A BASIC GRID, FIVE SQUARES WIDE AND THREE SQUARES HIGH. USE THE GRID TO HELP YOU SKETCH LINES FOR THE BODY, FINS, AND TAIL.

2

NEXT, USE A SOFT PENCIL TO SKETCH THE ROUGH OUTLINE. DRAW LINES TO SHOW THE SHAPE OF THE MOUTH AND THROAT, AND ADD A CIRCLE FOR THE EYE.

3

USE GRAY AND BLUE WATERCOLOR. THEN ADD HIGHLIGHTS WITH GRAY AND BLUE PENCILS. USE BLACK FOR DETAILS, SUCH AS THE EYE AND BUMPS ON THE HEAD.

A humpback's head and lower jaw are covered with bumps, called tubercles, which are hair follicles!

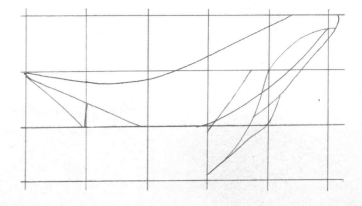

KILLER WHALE

1

DRAW A GRID, THREE SQUARES WIDE AND FIVE SQUARES HIGH. USING IT AS A GUIDE, ADD LINES FOR THE BODY, FINS, AND TAIL.

Killer whale calves are born with a yellowish tinge to their skin, which fades to white over time!

2

FIRM UP THE OUTLINE. ADD LINES TO SHOW WHERE THE WHITE AREAS WILL BE. DRAW AN EYE BETWEEN THE WHITE MARKINGS ON THE FACE.

3

COLOR USING BLACK AND WHITE PAINT FOR THE BODY, WITH GRAY AND WHITE FOR HIGHLIGHTS, SHADING, AND SPLASHES OF WATER!

MANDRILL

MANDRILLS ARE THE LARGEST AND MOST COLORFUL OF THE MONKEYS. FOLLOW THESE STEPS TO DRAW YOUR OWN!

Mandrills have colorful red and blue bottoms that are used to attract a mate. Try using highlighter pens!

1
START BY SKETCHING A LARGE OVAL FOR THE BODY AND A CIRCLE FOR THE HEAD. ADD FOUR BASIC SAUSAGE SHAPES FOR THE LIMBS.

2
WORK UP THE OUTLINE, ADDING FEET AND A TAIL. SKETCH IN THE FACE—A T-SHAPED BROW AND EGG-SHAPED MUZZLE.

3
FURTHER DEFINE THE FACE WITH A SOFT PENCIL. USE CROSSHATCHING TO ADD DARK SHADING AROUND THE EYES AND CHEEKS.

4

COLOR YOUR MANDRILL WITH
BROWN AND BLACK PENCILS ON
THE BODY, AND YELLOWS, REDS,
AND BLUES FOR THE FACE.

Mandrill males
can measure up
to 3 ft in height
and weigh as
much as 70 lb!

GERBIL

Gerbils have a natural instinct to burrow. When kept as pets, they like to make nests from straw, paper, and wood shavings!

1

DRAW TWO CIRCLES FOR THE HEAD AND BODY. ADD LEGS AND THE TAIL.

HAMSTER

A hamster's diet usually consists of seeds, grains, nuts, vegetables, and fruits, but they will eat some meats.

1

SKETCH TWO OVALS FOR THE HEAD AND BODY. ADD THREE ROUGH LEGS.

MOUSE

Mice are curious animals who love to explore and investigate. Pet mice should have ladders and wheels in their cages.

1

DRAW TWO OVALS FOR THE HEAD AND BODY. ADD THREE ROUGH LEGS.

2

SKETCH IN THE
OUTLINE AND ADD
EARS, EYES, NOSE,
AND PAWS.

3

COLOR WITH BROWN
AND GRAY PENCILS,
ADDING LOTS OF LINES
TO SHOW THE FUR.

2

ADD AN EAR, NOSE, AND
MOUTH, AS WELL AS A
ROUGH STRAWBERRY.

3

USE BROWN, ORANGE, YELLOW,
AND WHITE PENCILS TO COLOR.
ADD PINK TO THE EARS AND NOSE.

2

PENCIL IN THE
OUTLINE AND ADD
A NOSE, EYE, EARS,
AND A TAIL.

3

COLOR WITH BROWN,
GRAY AND YELLOW
PENCILS. ADD PINK
FOR THE EARS.

LEOPARD

1

SKETCH A SERIES OF OVERLAPPING OBLONGS TO CREATE THE BODY AND HEAD. ADD SAUSAGE SHAPES FOR THE LIMBS.

2

USING A SOFT PENCIL, SKETCH THE OVERALL OUTLINE. THEN ADD A TAIL AND DETAIL TO ITS FACE, LEGS, AND EARS.

3

TO COLOR, USE BROWN, ORANGE, YELLOW, AND WHITE PAINTS. USE A BLACK PENCIL TO DEFINE THE FACE AND ADD SPOTS.

1

DRAW OVERLAPPING CIRCLES AND OVALS FOR THE HEAD AND BODY, AND LONG SAUSAGE SHAPES FOR THE BENT LEGS.

2

NOW USE A SOFT PENCIL TO COMPLETE THE OUTLINE AND ADD DETAIL, INCLUDING TAIL, LEGS, AND FACE SHAPE.

3

COLOR WITH BROWN, ORANGE, AND YELLOW PENCILS. USE A BLACK PENCIL TO DEFINE THE FACE AND ADD SPOTS.

Leopards are excellent climbers. They often climb trees to rest on the branches, and descend head first!

SQUIRREL

GRAY SQUIRRELS MAKE THEIR NESTS, OR DRAYS, IN TALL TREES, STORING NUTS INSIDE THEM, READY TO EAT LATER!

1

START WITH A LARGE SQUASHED OVAL FOR THE BODY AND TWO SMALLER OVALS FOR THE PAWS AND FEET. DRAW A CURVED LINE FOR THE TAIL.

2

USING THE GUIDE SHAPES, FIRM UP THE OUTLINE OF THE SQUIRREL. ADD EARS AND EYES TO ITS FACE, CLAWS TO ITS FEET, AND A NUT IN ITS PAWS.

3

TO COLOR, USE BROWN, GRAY, AND WHITE PENCILS, WITH A LITTLE BLACK FOR THE EYE AND CLAWS. USE RED AND BROWN FOR THE NUT.

Gray squirrels aren't fussy eaters—they eat seeds, buds, flowers, shoots, nuts, berries, eggs, fungi, insects, small birds, and amphibians!

PERSIAN CAT

THIS LONGHAIRED CAT IS A FUSSY EATER THAT LIKES PLENTY OF GROOMING. DRAW YOUR OWN PAMPERED PUSS!

1 FIRST, DRAW A LARGE SQUASHED CIRCLE FOR THE CAT'S HEAD. THEN SKETCH A LARGER CIRCLE FOR ITS BODY AND A SQUASHED OBLONG FOR ITS BUSHY TAIL.

2 NOW WORK UP THE OUTLINE OF THE CAT USING THE BASIC SHAPES. ADD SMALL CIRCLES TO THE CAT'S FACE FOR ITS EYES, NOSE, AND MOUTH. SKETCH IN THE PAWS AND ADD EARS.

3 ADD FUR ALL OVER WITH A SOFT PENCIL. TRY FEATHERING YOUR STROKES TO MAKE YOUR CAT LOOK FLUFFY. SKETCH IN DETAILS TO THE FACE AND PAWS.

Persian cats have a furry ruff around their necks, long ear and toe tufts, and a full "brush" tail!

4 ALTHOUGH THIS CAT IS WHITE, YOU CAN USE SUBTLE SHADES OF YELLOW AND GRAY TO PAINT IT. COLOR ITS EYES BRIGHT GREEN AND ADD A LITTLE PINK TO THE TIP OF ITS NOSE AND TONGUE.

PANDA

GIANT PANDAS LOVE BAMBOO! THEY CAN SPEND UP TO 12 HOURS A DAY EATING THE STUFF. DRAW YOUR OWN PANDA MUNCHING ON ITS FAVORITE FOOD!

1

DRAW A CIRCLE FOR THE HEAD, WITH TWO EYE PATCHES AND A NOSE. ADD A U-SHAPED BODY AND GUIDELINES FOR THE LEGS.

2

SKETCH UPSIDE-DOWN U-SHAPED LINES FOR THE EARS. THEN WORK UP THE EYES AND NOSE. CREATE THE ARMS AND PAWS.

3

USING THE GUIDES, BREAK THE LINES UP TO ILLUSTRATE FUR. ADD SOME TUFTS OF GRASS UNDERNEATH THE PANDA.

4

ADD A FEW BRANCHES OF BAMBOO COMING OUT OF ITS MOUTH AND SOME IN ITS PAWS AND LAP. THEN BEGIN SHADING.

5

USE A LIGHT GRAY
WATERCOLOR WASH ON
THE MAIN BODY, WITH
LIGHTER GRAY AND WHITE
HIGHLIGHTS. USE A
BLACK PENCIL TO CREATE
FUR TEXTURE ALL OVER.

Pandas eat
18-36 lb of
bamboo every
day, while
sitting upright!

HIPPOPOTAMUS

THESE CREATURES LOVE WATER, WHICH IS WHY THE ANCIENT GREEKS NAMED THEM "HIPPOPOTAMUS" MEANING "RIVER HORSE." DRAW YOURS NEXT TO A RIVER!

1

START WITH AN OVAL BODY AND FOUR OVAL LEGS. DRAW A CIRCLE FOR THE HEAD, THEN TWO OVALS FOR THE TOP AND BOTTOM JAWS— JOIN WITH A C-SHAPED GUIDELINE. ADD AN EAR AND EYE.

2

USING THE GUIDE SHAPES, CREATE A SOLID OUTLINE. ADD THE HIPPO'S PUPIL, INNER EAR, AND TEETH—LITTLE ONES AT THE TOP AND BIG ONES AT THE BOTTOM—AND TOES TO THE FEET.

3

HIPPOS ARE VERY WRINKLY, SO
GO OVER THE OUTLINE AND ADD
LOTS OF CREASES AND FOLDS TO
ITS SKIN. ADD A SMALL STUBBY
TAIL AND SHADOWS UNDER THE
STOMACH AND IN THE MOUTH.

A hippo's jaw hinge is
so far back that it
can open its mouth to
almost 150 degrees!

4

PAINT USING A LIGHT BROWN
AND GRAY FOR THE BODY AND
PINK FOR INSIDE ITS MOUTH.
ADD ROUGH SHADING TO SHOW
THE HIPPO'S SKIN, AND WHITE
PAINT ON ITS TEETH AND EYE.

KANGAROO

1

DRAW A LARGE CIRCLE, WITH AN OVAL INSIDE IT FOR THE BODY. ADD A SMALL OVAL HEAD AND GUIDELINES FOR THE NECK, TAIL, AND LEGS.

2

REFINE THE SHAPE OF THE HEAD AND DRAW SOME EARS. PENCIL IN THE KANGAROO'S LARGE HIND LEGS, TWO SMALLER FOLDED FRONT LEGS, AND TAIL.

3

NOW ADD SOME DETAILS TO THE FACE, INCLUDING THE EYE, NOSE, AND MOUTH. SKETCH IN A BIT OF MUSCLE DEFINITION TO THE LEGS AND SHOULDER AREAS.

1

DRAW AN OVAL FOR THE LOWER BODY AND AN EGG SHAPE FOR THE UPPER BODY. DRAW TWO CIRCLE HEADS— ONE FOR THE MOTHER, ONE FOR THE JOEY. ADD AN OVAL FOR THE HIP OF THE HIND LEG.

2

WITH A SOFT PENCIL USE THE GUIDE SHAPES TO FIRM UP THE OVERALL OUTLINE. ADD ARMS, LEGS, AND A TAIL. SKETCH DETAILS TO EACH FACE, INCLUDING EARS, AND ADD THE JOEY'S ARMS.

4

COLOR WITH A BROWN WATERCOLOR WASH. ADD DARKER TONES OF BROWNS AND A LITTLE GRAY. USE BLACK TO ADD IN THE EYES AND NOSE.

Kangaroos move at speeds of up to 35 mph by jumping using their powerful hind legs!

3

REFINE THE SHAPE OF THE KANGAROO, NARROWING THE UPPER BODY AND HEAD. COMPLETE THE FACE BY ADDING LINES AND SHADING. ADD LINES TO SHOW MUSCLES AND FUR TEXTURE.

4

COLOR WITH LIGHT AND DARK SHADES OF BROWN. ADD FACE DETAILS IN GRAY AND BLACK AND A FEW FUR HIGHLIGHTS USING A WHITE PEN OR PAINT.

DrAGONFLY

THIS GREEN DARNER DRAGONFLY HAS A WINGSPAN OF 3 IN! DRAW YOURS ACTUAL SIZE, OR SCALE IT UP FOR A ZOOMED-IN PICTURE.

1

START WITH AN ANGLED RECTANGLE, THEN SKETCH A SAUSAGE SHAPE FOR THE BODY, WITH A SMALL CIRCLE FOR THE HEAD.

2

SKETCH FOUR ELONGATED LEAF SHAPES POINTING TOWARD THE BODY. ADD A CURVED LINE AT THE TOP OF THE SAUSAGE SHAPE.

3

DIVIDE THE HEAD INTO TWO EYES. ADD DETAIL TO THE BODY BY SHAPING THE ABDOMEN AND ADDING LINES TO SHOW SEGMENTS.

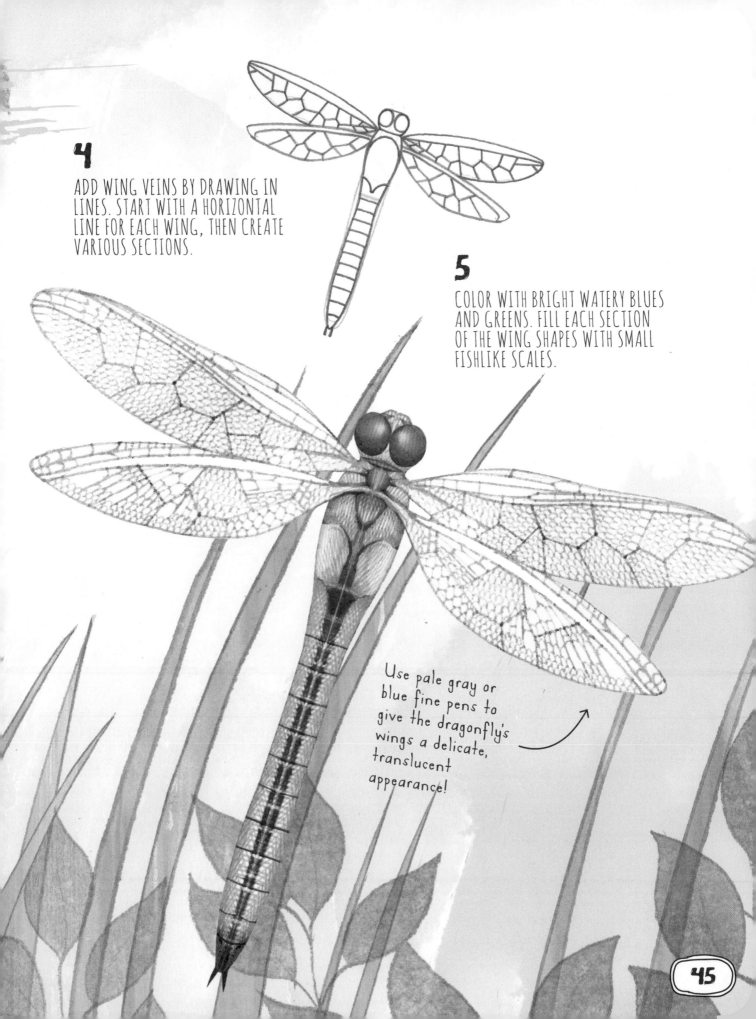

4

ADD WING VEINS BY DRAWING IN LINES. START WITH A HORIZONTAL LINE FOR EACH WING, THEN CREATE VARIOUS SECTIONS.

5

COLOR WITH BRIGHT WATERY BLUES AND GREENS. FILL EACH SECTION OF THE WING SHAPES WITH SMALL FISHLIKE SCALES.

Use pale gray or blue fine pens to give the dragonfly's wings a delicate, translucent appearance!

SEA LION

1 DRAW THREE SQUASHED OVALS STACKED ON TOP OF EACH OTHER. THESE WILL FORM THE HEAD, LONG NECK, AND LARGE BODY.

2 USE A SOFT PENCIL TO SKETCH THE OVERALL OUTLINE. ADD IN BASIC SHAPES FOR ITS FRONT AND BACK FLIPPERS.

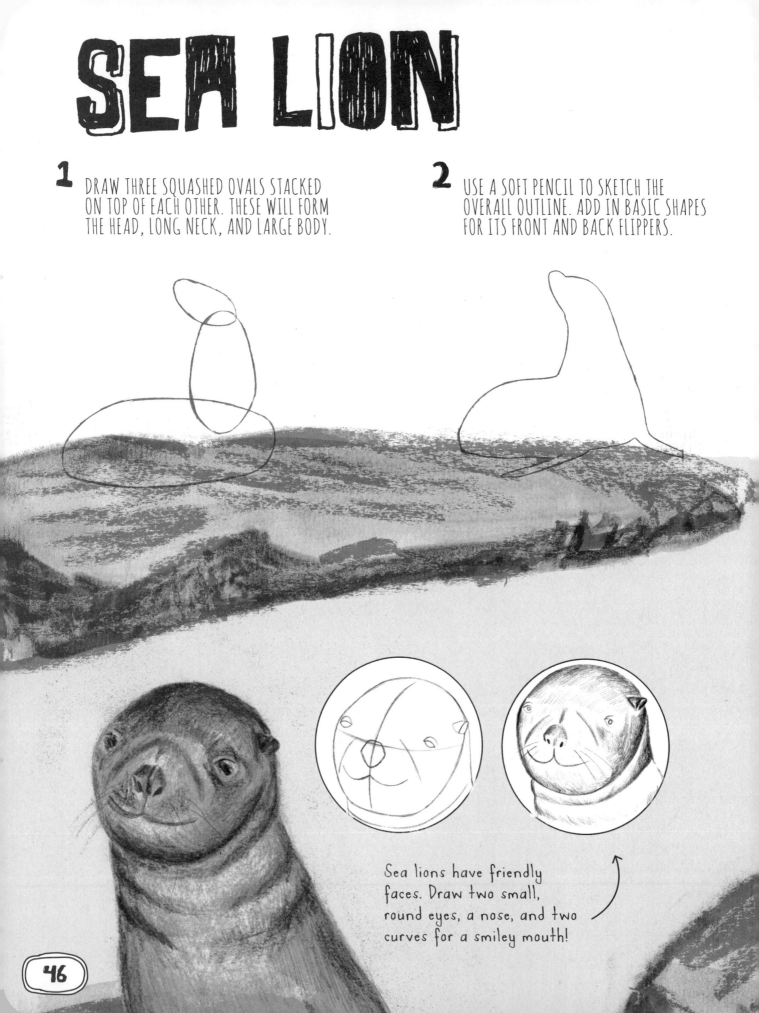

Sea lions have friendly faces. Draw two small, round eyes, a nose, and two curves for a smiley mouth!

CALIFORNIA SEA LIONS HAVE LONG TORPEDO-SHAPED BODIES THAT ARE WELL DESIGNED FOR MOVEMENT BOTH IN THE WATER AND ON LAND!

3 ADD DETAILS, INCLUDING A NOSE, MOUTH, EYE, AND CREASE LINES ON THE NECK AND STOMACH.

4 COLOR WITH A BLACK WASH, THEN ADD BROWN, YELLOW, AND WHITE PENCIL HIGHLIGHTS AND BLACK WHISKERS.

Even when out of water, sea lions have shiny, smooth fur. Add lots of highlights to show this effect!

ARCTIC WOLF

1

BEGIN BY DRAWING THREE OVALS—TWO OVERLAPPING FOR THE BODY AND HIND LEGS, AND ONE FOR THE HEAD.

2

USING A SOFT PENCIL, JOIN THE GUIDE SHAPES WITH A SMOOTH OUTLINE, ADDING THE BASIC SHAPES OF THE WOLF'S MUZZLE.

3

USE ROUGH CIRCLES TO SHOW THE SHOULDER AND HIP POSITIONS, THEN ADD THE LEGS FROM THERE. FOLLOW WITH A BUSHY TAIL.

Wolves howl to communicate with each other. Their calls can be heard up to 3 mi away!

4

ADD DETAILS TO THE FACE, EAR, AND MOUTH. THE FUR SHOULD BE SMOOTH ON THE WOLF'S BACK, BUT RUFFLED AROUND ITS NECK.

5

THE WOLF HAS WHITE FUR, BUT USE BLUE AND GRAY PENCILS TO SHOW HOW THE SNOW REFLECTS OFF IT.

FARM BIRDS

GOOSE

Start with a circle for the body and a small circle for the head. Connect with curved lines for the neck. Add a beak, eye, legs, feet, and feathers. Paint white, with orange for the beak and feet.

A female is called a goose and a male is called a gander.

DUCK

Draw a squashed oval for the body and a small oval head. Add a beak, eye, legs, feet, and feathers. Paint white and gray, with an orange and red beak, and orange feet.

Ducks have highly waterproof feathers. Even when underwater, the underlayer stays dry!

TURKEY

Draw two large ovals for the body and tail, and a small circle for the head. Sketch two lines for the neck. Add an eye, beak, jowls, and feet. Color with black, brown, gray, blue, and red pencils.

The skin on a turkey's throat and head can change color when the bird is distressed or excited!

CHICKEN

Sketch circles for the head and body. Connect with curved lines for the neck. Add an eye, beak, wing, feathers, tail, and feet. Color with black, brown, gray, red, and yellow pencils.

Male chickens are bigger and more brightly colored than females.

LION

THIS ENDANGERED SPECIES OF WEST AFRICAN LION IS SMALLER THAN LIONS FROM SOUTHERN AFRICA, AND IS ON THE VERGE OF EXTINCTION.

1

DRAW A SQUASHED CIRCLE FOR THE FRONT OF THE BODY AND A CURVED LINE FOR THE BACK. ADD A CIRCLE FOR THE HEAD, AND LINES FOR THE NECK AND LEGS.

2

USING THE BASIC SHAPES AND LINES AS A GUIDE, WORK UP THE BUSHY MANE, ROUGH FACIAL FEATURES, BODY, RECTANGULAR LEGS, ROUGH FEET, AND TAIL.

Once you've completed your lion drawing, you could try your hand at a lioness!

When drawing lion cubs, keep fur fluffier!

3

NOW ADD THE DETAIL TO THE LION. SKETCH IN ITS EYES, NOSE, MOUTH, EAR, AND LINES ON ITS PAWS. USE A SOFT PENCIL TO ADD HAIR, THEN SMUDGE IT FOR A FUR EFFECT.

4

FOR THE COLORING STAGE, USE SHADES OF BROWN WITH A LITTLE YELLOW AND ORANGE FOR THE LION'S FUR. USE A SHARP BLACK PENCIL TO DEFINE THE FACIAL FEATURES.

BUTTERFLY

LEARN TO DRAW A MONARCH BUTTERFLY! TRY SKETCHING IT ON BLUE PAPER FOR A CLEAR SKY, THEN ADD A COLORFUL MEADOW BENEATH.

1

START WITH A VERTICAL LINE. SKETCH A CIRCLE FOR THE HEAD, TWO CIRCLES FOR THE THORAX, AND A SQUASHED OVAL FOR THE ABDOMEN. ADD IN THE TOP AND BOTTOM PARTS OF THE WINGS.

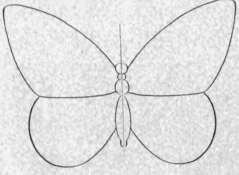

2

PENCIL IN THE FLUTED SHAPES OF THE WINGS AND ADD A ROUGH WING PATTERN, INCLUDING SPOTS AROUND THE OUTER EDGES. ADD LINES FOR ANTENNAE AND DETAIL TO THE HEAD AND BODY.

BUTTERFLIES HAVE ALL SORTS OF INTRICATE AND COLORFUL WING PATTERNS. HERE ARE A FEW OTHER EXAMPLES TO TRY.

GIANT SWALLOWTAIL

This large butterfly has an average wingspan of 5 in. The wings are black with yellow bands.

AMERICAN PAINTED LADY

The painted lady has reddish-orange wings, with brown edging and white spots. It has a wingspan of 2 in.

3

PAINT THE BUTTERFLY'S BODY BLACK. TO
CREATE THE FADED ORANGE LOOK, ADD
A WASH OF YELLOW FIRST, THEN LAYER
ORANGE OVER THE TOP.

To draw a monarch
butterfly from the side,
sketch the basic shape
of the wings, with one
overlapping the other.

JAY

Start with a basic shape for the outline of the feather. Make fine pencil lines to show textures. Color with a gray watercolor wash and use black, blue, and white pencils for highlights.

PARAKEET

Sketch out a rough sausage shape for the outline of the feather. Add in the pattern with a soft pencil. Color it green and yellow with dark brown areas. Use a sharp black pencil to add details.

PEACOCK

This feather has an almost flowerlike shape to it. Make a basic outline for the main area, with small feathery branches below. Color the feather with black, greens, blues, browns, and yellows.

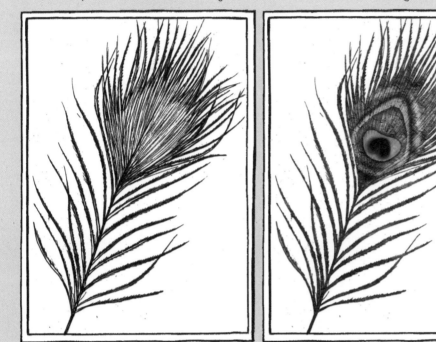

Jay

Parakeet

Peacock

QUAIL

These small quail feathers are a rough teardrop shape. Use a soft pencil for the outline and a dark brown pencil for the main color. Add cream spots and a fluffy outline.

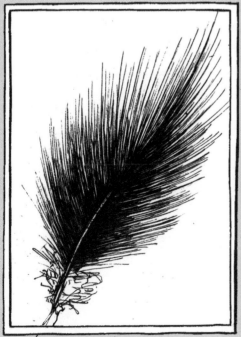

Quail

LEMUR

LEMURS MOVE ACROSS THE GROUND BY STANDING UPRIGHT AND HOPPING SIDEWAYS, WITH THEIR ARMS HELD OUT. IT LOOKS AS IF THEY ARE DANCING. DRAW YOUR OWN LEAPING LEMUR!

1

DRAW A LONG OVAL FOR THE BODY, WITH A CIRCLE ON TOP FOR THE HEAD. PENCIL IN ELONGATED HEART SHAPES FOR THE LEMUR'S LIMBS.

2

ADD SMALL OVALS AT THE END OF EACH LIMB. MARK OUT A SMALL MUZZLE AND ROUND EYES WITHIN A HEART-SHAPED FACE. ADD A TINY OVAL FOR THE EAR.

3

CONNECT THE SHAPES WITH A FLUID LINE. DRAW IN SOME HANDS, FEET, AND A LONG TAIL. ADD SHADING TO THE HANDS AND FEET WITH A SOFT PENCIL.

4

COLOR THE BODY WITH A PALE
SANDY WATERCOLOR WASH.
USE PENCILS TO SHADE THE CHEST
AND HANDS DARK GRAY. ADD A
BLACK FACE WITH YELLOW EYES.

Lemurs are native
to the island of
Madagascar, so complete
your drawing with a
rainforest backdrop!

DEER

1

DRAW A BEAN SHAPE AS A GUIDE FOR THE BODY, TWO OVALS FOR THE NECK, SAUSAGE SHAPES TO MAKE UP THE LEGS, AND A POINTED OVAL FOR THE HEAD.

2

USING THE GUIDE SHAPES, SKETCH AN OUTLINE FOR EACH DEER. ADD TWO ROUGH TRIANGLES FOR THE EARS AND FOUR ROUGH SQUARES FOR THE HOOVES.

3

ERASE THE UNNECESSARY GUIDELINES. DRAW THE EYES AND NOSE. THEN FURTHER DEFINE THE OUTLINE OF THE DEER, INCLUDING THE TAIL.

4

SHADE IN THE EYES, EARS, NOSE, AND HOOVES, THEN ROUGHLY PENCIL IN AREAS OF LIGHTER AND DARKER FUR ON EACH DEER'S COAT.

5

WITH A COLORED PEN, PENCIL, OR PAINTS, USE SOFT STROKES FOR THE FUR. ADD FINAL DETAILS TO THE EYES, EARS, AND NOSE WITH A SHARP PENCIL.

Most fallow deer have a chestnut-colored, white-spotted coat, but on some the spots are not very prominent and may disappear in winter.

61

BEETLE

DUNG BEETLE

1

START BY DRAWING THREE LARGE CIRCLES— ONE EACH FOR THE BEETLE'S HEAD, THORAX, AND ABDOMEN.

2

NEXT, USE A SOFT PENCIL TO SKETCH IN THE BEETLE'S FOUR SEGMENTED BACK LEGS AND TWO FRONT LEGS.

3

COLOR YOUR BEETLE USING BLACK PENCILS. SUBTLE HIGHLIGHTS CAN BE ADDED WITH WHITE PENCILS.

Once you've drawn your beetle, add a ball of dung for it to roll. Dung beetles will bury their ball, and eat it later or lay their eggs in it!

LADYBUG

1
DRAW A LARGE OVAL FOR THE LADYBUG'S ABDOMEN AND ATTACH TWO SMALLER OVALS FOR ITS HEAD AND THORAX.

2
DRAW A HORIZONTAL LINE TO DIVIDE THE WINGS. ROUGHLY SKETCH IN THE LADYBUG'S FEATURES AND LEGS.

3
COMPLETE YOUR DRAW
WITH BRIGHT RED WINGS,
AND BLACK LEGS AND HEAD.
LEAVE SOME BITS WHITE.

STAG BEETLE

1
DRAW A POINTED OVAL FOR THE BODY AND TWO SMALLER OVALS FOR THE HEAD AND THORAX. ADD LARGE PINCERS.

2
ADD IN MORE DETAIL TO THE BODY AND HEAD. PENCIL SIX THIN LEGS AND TWO TINY FRONT ANTENNAE.

3
USE BLACK AND BROWN PENCILS FOR YOUR STAG BEETLE, WITH SUBTLE ORANGE HIGHLIGHTS.

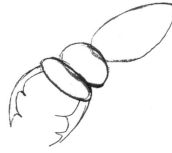

Stag beetles use their huge jaws to wrestle other males over females. Once you've mastered one, add another beetle for it to fight!

SCARLET MACAW

A MACAW IS A LARGE, LONG-TAILED PARROT. DRAW YOUR SCARLET MACAW IN THE TROPICAL RAINFORESTS OF SOUTH AMERICA!

1

DRAW A LARGE OVAL FOR THE BODY AND A SMALL CIRCLE ON TOP FOR THE HEAD. THEN ADD A LONG U-SHAPED TAIL.

2

USE THE GUIDE SHAPES TO DRAW THE OUTLINE. DRAW A BEAK, EYES, FEET, AND WINGS. THEN ADD BASIC FEATHER LINES.

3

ADD DETAILS TO THE FACE AND SHADE THE SIDES OF THE BEAK. BUILD UP THE FEATHERS, WORKING DOWN FROM THE TOP.

4

PAINT THE HEAD, BODY, WING TOPS, AND TAIL RED. ADD BANDS OF YELLOW AND BLUE IN THE MIDDLE OF THE WINGS AND BLACK ON THE FACE.

FEATHERS

Add texture to the feathers by drawing a line down the center of each one, then adding some lighter lines coming out and downward at an angle.

CAPUCHIN MONKEY

1

START BY DRAWING A SLIGHTLY SQUASHED CIRCLE FOR THE FACE. MARK OUT THE EARS AND SHOULDERS.

Capuchin monkeys are so called because they look like Spanish Capuchin monks, with white faces and brown robes!

2

ADD A HEART-SHAPED OUTLINE FOR ITS FACE, THEN SKETCH IN THE EYES, NOSTRILS, MOUTH, AND EAR DETAIL.

3

COLOR WITH A MIX OF BROWNS, GRAY AND A LITTLE PINK. ADD BLACK TO THE EYES, WITH WHITE HIGHLIGHTS.

3

COLOR THE BODY BLACK AND THE CHEST AND SHOULDERS WHITE. ADD A TOUCH OF PINK TO THE FACE.

2

NOW FIRM UP THE OUTLINE, ADDING IN SOME DETAIL TO THE BODY SHAPE. SKETCH A BASIC HEART SHAPE FOR THE FACE.

1

SKETCH A LARGE OVAL FOR THE BODY, A CIRCLE FOR THE HEAD, AND LONG SAUSAGE SHAPES FOR THE ARMS, LEGS AND TAIL.

Capuchins spend most of their time in the treetops, where they can find food, away from predators.

POSSUM

THE COMMON BRUSHTAIL POSSUM IS A SMALL NOCTURNAL ANIMAL THAT USES ITS LONG, BUSHY TAIL TO GRIP ONTO BRANCHES!

1

DRAW A CIRCLE FOR THE HEAD, FOLLOWED BY THREE SMALL CIRCLES FOR THE EYES AND NOSE. ADD U-SHAPED EARS AND AN ALMOND-SHAPED BODY.

2

SKETCH GUIDE SHAPES FOR THE LEGS, FEET, AND TAIL. PENCIL IN A ROUGH BRANCH SHAPE ABOVE THE POSSUM. WRAP ITS TAIL AROUND THE BRANCH.

3

USING THE GUIDES, DRAW THE OUTLINE OF YOUR POSSUM. ADD SMALL TOES TO EACH FOOT. TRY TO BREAK UP THE LINES TO SHOW THE FUR.

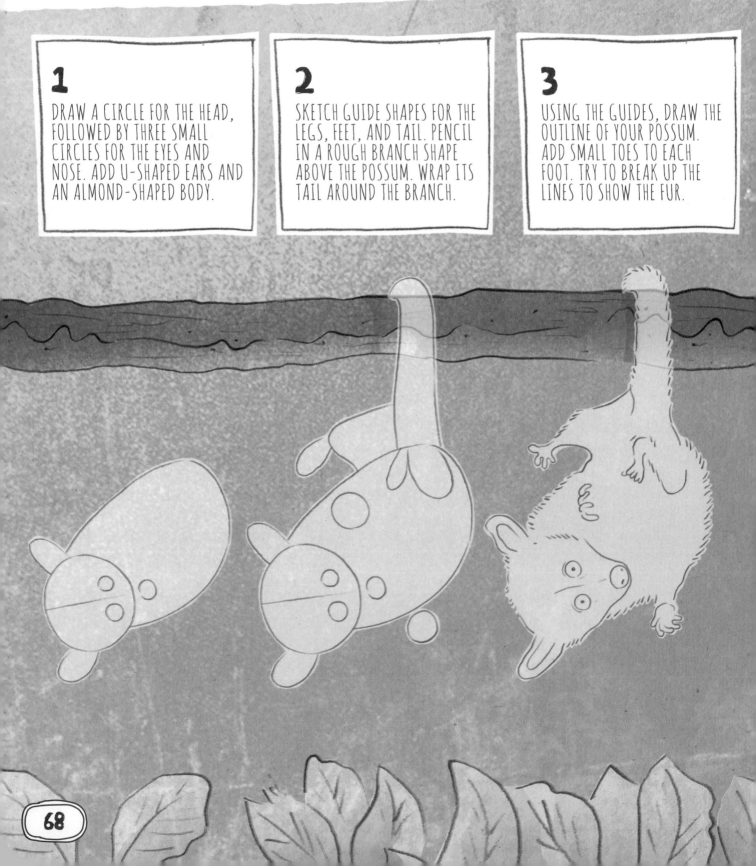

4

USE BROWN AND GRAY PAINT FOR THE BODY, AND PINK FOR THE NOSE AND FEET. USE A BLACK PENCIL FOR SHADING AND WHITE FOR HIGHLIGHTS.

Common brushtail possums have large, pointed ears.

Possums spend most of their lives—living, eating, and sleeping—in tall trees.

TROPICAL FISH

ORANGE CLOWNFISH

A clownfish has three white lines across its bright orange body. Each fin has a black edging.

1

START WITH AN OVAL FOR THE BASIC BODY OF THE FISH. ADD A HORIZONTAL GUIDELINE AND ROUGH TAIL FIN.

2

BELOW THE GUIDELINE, ADD A C-SHAPED PECTORAL FIN. THEN ADD TWO FLAT DORSAL FINS AND AN ANAL FIN.

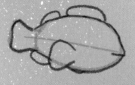

COPPER BUTTERFLYFISH

This fish is also known as "beaked coralfish," because of its snout. It has a distinctive eye-spot on its dorsal fin.

1

DRAW A CIRCLE WITH A POINTED END FOR THE BODY. ADD A HORIZONTAL GUIDELINE AND ROUGH TAIL FIN.

2

ADD A V-SHAPED DORSAL FIN, AND SMALLER V-SHAPED ANAL FIN. DRAW TRIANGULAR PECTORAL FINS AND A DOT FOR THE EYE.

PENNANT CORALFISH

These fish are mostly black and white, with elongated dorsal fins. Their fins can be bright yellow.

1

SKETCH A CIRCLE WITH A POINTED END FOR THE BODY, A LINE FOR THE DORSAL FIN, AND TRIANGLES FOR THE OTHER FINS.

2

USING THE GUIDE SHAPES, FIRM UP THE OUTLINE OF THE FISH. ADD AN EYE AND ROUGH STRIPE PATTERN.

3

COLOR WITH YELLOW AND ORANGE FIRST, THEN ADD THE WHITE STRIPES. COLOR THE EDGE OF THE FINS WITH BLACK.

3

COLOR THE STRIPES WITH YELLOW AND ORANGE. ADD GRAY TO THE WHITE SECTIONS AND A BLACK EYE.

3

COLOR THE FISH WITH BLACK AND YELLOW STRIPES, ADDING GRAY HIGHLIGHTS TO THE WHITE STRIPES.

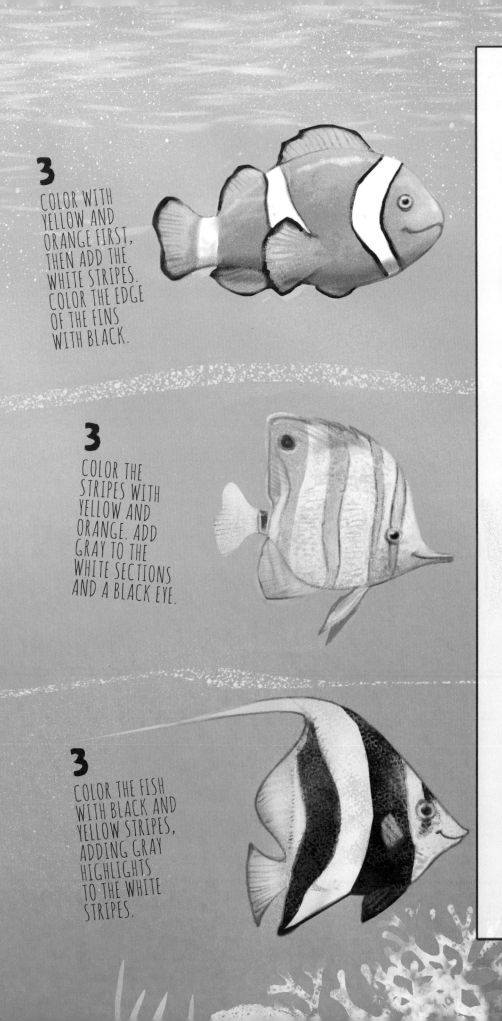

CORAL

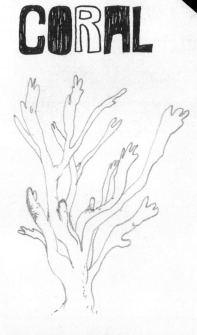

Draw the rough shape of the coral, adding plenty of varied twisting branch shapes.

Paint a flat color and then sprinkle sea salt onto the wet picture for a coral effect!

rABBIT

1

DRAW A LARGE CIRCLE AND A SMALLER CIRCLE. THE LARGE CIRCLE WILL FORM THE BODY OF THE RABBIT AND THE SMALL ONE WILL FORM THE HEAD.

2

JOIN THE TWO CIRCLES TOGETHER WITH CURVED LINES. CREATE THE NOSE BY ADDING A CURVED POINT TO THE SMALLER CIRCLE.

3

DRAW TWO CARROT SHAPES ON TOP OF THE HEAD FOR THE EARS. ADD ANOTHER UNDER THE LARGER CIRCLE FOR THE BACK LEG. ADD TWO FORELEGS.

4

NOW START TO FILL IN DETAILS. SKETCH THE INSIDE OF THE RABBIT'S EAR, NOSE, MOUTH, AND EYES. DON'T FORGET TO ADD A FLUFFY TAIL, TOO!

5

USING A SMALL BRUSH OR PENCIL, ADD LOTS OF
FLUFFY FUR LINES ALL OVER THE RABBIT'S BODY
AND TO SOFTEN THE OUTLINE.

6

USE PENCILS OR PAINT TO
COMPLETE YOUR RABBIT. TRY
LOTS OF DIFFERENT COLORS
INCLUDING BEIGE, WHITE,
BROWN, AND BLACK.

Be playful with where
you place the ears.
Some rabbits' ears point
down, while others
stick straight up!

EMPEROR TAMARIN

Draw an upside-down U-shaped line for the head, with triangular ears, circular eyes, and a semicircle snout. Add a large, curved mustache and beard lines. Shade with black pencils and add gray, pink, and white highlights.

COMMON MARMOSET

Sketch a squashed circle for the head, with three lines for each ear tuft. Add rough eye markings and facial details. Color with brown, gray, and pink pencils. Use white for the ear tufts.

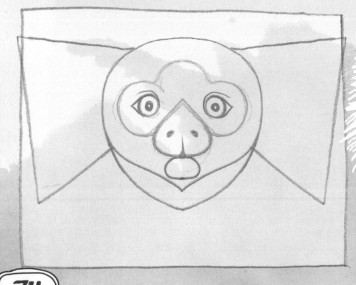

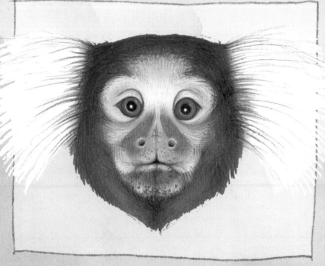

SPIDER MONKEY

Draw a circular head and a curved line for the brow and ear tufts. Add circles for eyes, an oval muzzle, and lines for facial markings. Color with brown, orange, and yellow pencils.

THERE ARE 264 KNOWN SPECIES OF MONKEY. THE LARGEST IS THE MANDRILL, WEIGHING 70 LB, WHILE THE SMALLEST IS THE PYGMY MARMOSET AT JUST 5 OZ!

SQUIRREL MONKEY

Start with an egg-shaped head, oval muzzle, and circular eye patches. Add curved lines for the ears. Work up the facial details. Color with brown, orange, and gray pencils.

TOAD

1 DRAW A SQUASHED EGG SHAPE FOR THE TOAD'S BODY. ADD A LARGE CIRCLE FOR ITS BULGING THROAT.

2 NEXT, PENCIL IN THE EYES. THEN ADD THE LEGS AND FEET WITH CIRCULAR TIPS ON EACH TOE.

3 COLOR WITH A BROWN AND ORANGE WASH. ADD WARTS AND CREASES TO THE SKIN WITH BROWN AND ORANGE PENCILS.

Toads breathe air in through their nostrils, making their throats bulge. Keep colors light to show the transparency of the stretched skin!

FROG

1 START WITH A VERTICAL SQUASHED OVAL FOR THE FROG'S BODY. THEN ADD THE LEGS AND FEET.

2 NOW ADD MORE DETAIL, INCLUDING TWO BULGING EYES, NOSTRILS, AND A WIDE MOUTH.

During extremely low temperatures, a wood frog can freeze! Its breathing and heartbeat stop, and start again when the ice melts.

3 COLOR YOUR DRAWING USING GREEN AND BROWN PAINT ON THE BODY. ADD YELLOW AND WHITE PENCIL HIGHLIGHTS.

GORILLA

1

START WITH THE MOTHER GORILLA—DRAW A CIRCLE FOR ITS TORSO AND AN OVERLAPPING OVAL FOR ITS HEAD. ADD A CIRCLE FOR ITS HIPS. NOW SKETCH A CIRCLE AND OVAL FOR THE BABY.

2

ADD IN SOME BASIC SAUSAGE SHAPES FOR THE GORILLA'S ARMS AND LEGS. THESE CAN BE QUITE ROUGH AT THIS STAGE. ADD THE BABY'S ARMS AND LEGS IN THE SAME WAY.

3

USING A SOFT PENCIL, GO AROUND THE OUTLINE OF BOTH THE MOTHER AND BABY GORILLA. BEGIN ADDING SOME SHAPE TO BOTH OF THEIR FACES, ARMS, AND HANDS.

4

NEXT, SKETCH DETAILS ON EACH FACE, INCLUDING EYES, NOSES, AND MOUTHS. USE THE SOFT PENCIL TO BEGIN BREAKING UP THE OUTLINE TO SHOW HAIR AND SKIN WRINKLES.

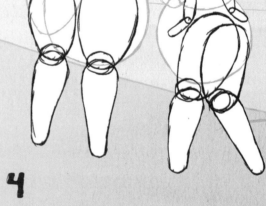

5

COLOR PRIMARILY WITH BLACK PAINTS AND PENCILS. USE BROWN AND GRAY TO ADD HIGHLIGHTS TO THE HAIR, AND WHITE AND BLUE TO ADD HIGHLIGHTS TO THE FACES.

Baby gorillas cling to their mother's back for safety from four months old, so add extra tufts of hair around the baby's hands!

79

1

DRAW A LARGE TEARDROP SHAPE FOR THE BODY AND A SMALL ONE FOR THE HEAD. JOIN WITH CURVED LINES. ADD A POINTED TAIL, AND VERTICAL CURVED LINES FOR WINGS.

2

FILL OUT THE BODY SHAPE AND ADD THE BEAK, FEET, AND FEATHER DETAIL TO THE TAIL. USING THE WING GUIDE, WORK UP THE OUTSTRETCHED WINGS.

3

DRAW AN EYE AND NOSTRIL ON THE FACE. ADD SOME FEATHER DETAIL TO THE WINGS, WITH SMALL C-SHAPED FEATHERS ON THE SIDE OF THE GOOSE'S BODY.

GOOSE

3

DRAW AN EYE AND NOSTRIL ON THE FACE. BUILD UP THE WING FEATHERS IN FIVE DIAGONAL STRIPS. ADD SMALL C-SHAPED FEATHERS ON THE BODY.

2

FILL OUT THE BODY SHAPE AND ADD THE BEAK, FEET, AND FEATHER DETAIL TO THE TAIL. USING THE WING GUIDE, WORK UP THE OUTSTRETCHED WINGS.

1

DRAW A LARGE TEARDROP SHAPE FOR THE BODY AND A SMALL ONE FOR THE HEAD. JOIN WITH CURVED LINES. ADD A POINTED TAIL AND DOWNWARD SLOPING LINES FOR WINGS.

4

USE GRAY AS A BASE AND BUILD UP THE COLOR FOR THE DARKER AREAS. ADD ORANGE TO THE BEAK AND FEET. USE A BLACK PENCIL TO ADD DETAILS.

Graylag geese fly in a V-formation. This allows them to fly farther for longer, as it cuts down on wind resistance!

4

START WITH LIGHT GRAY AS A BASE, THEN BUILD UP WITH DARKER GRAYS. ADD ORANGE FOR THE FEET AND BEAK. USE A BLACK PENCIL TO ADD DETAILS.

Show your geese in flight by placing them against a clear blue sky, with the ground far below!

RHINOCEROS

THE SOUTHERN WHITE RHINOCEROS IS THE LARGEST AND MOST NUMEROUS SPECIES. TRY DRAWING ONE!

1

START BY DRAWING A LARGE SQUASHED OVAL FOR THE BODY, WITH SMALLER OVALS FOR THE HEAD AND LEGS. ADD TWO BASIC HORNS.

White rhinos can weigh as much as 2 tons and stand as tall as 6 ft!

2

USE A SOFT PENCIL TO SKETCH A ROUGH OUTLINE FOR THE RHINOCEROS. ADD IN TWO EARS, AN EYE, AND TOES ON EACH FOOT.

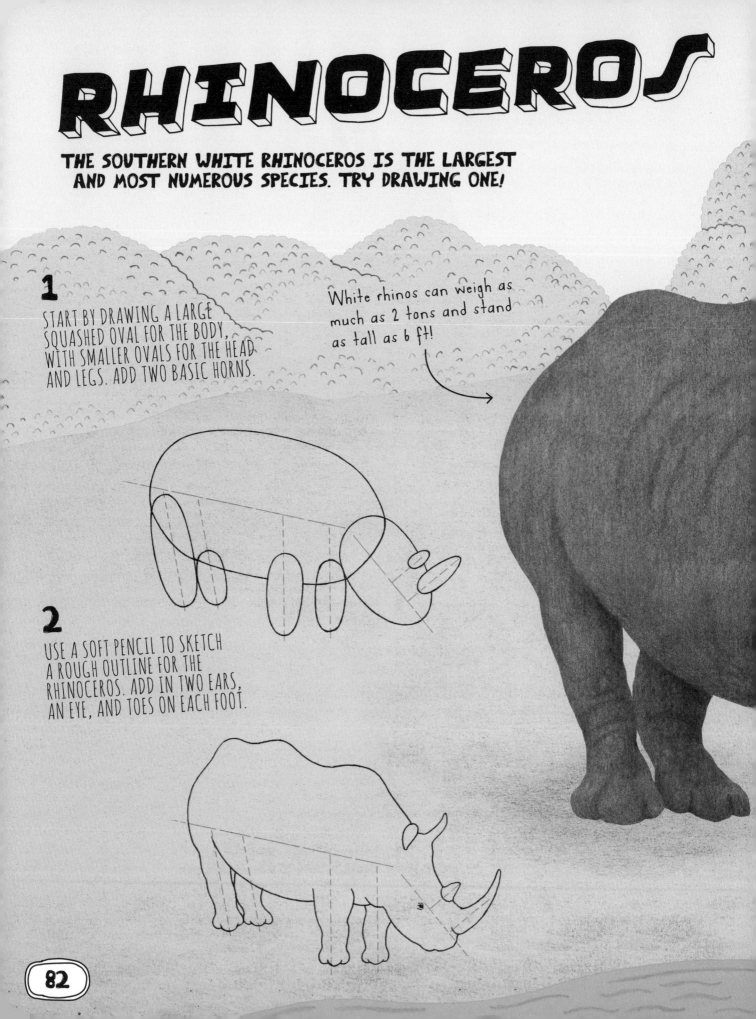

3

DRAW A COUPLE OF HORIZONTAL LINES ON EACH KNEE, TO SHOW SKIN WRINKLES. GIVE YOUR RHINO A LIGHT GRAY WATERCOLOR WASH.

White rhinos have two horns. The front horn is larger than the other, averaging 3 ft in length!

4

ADD SUBTLE SHADING WITH TOUCHES OF BLACK AND WHITE. USE A HARD PENCIL TO DEFINE ITS EYES, EARS, NOSTRIL, AND WRINKLES.

MOLE

1

DRAW A LARGE OVAL AS A GUIDE FOR
THE BODY, TWO OVALS FOR THE PAWS, A
CIRCLE FOR THE HEAD, AND A CONE SHAPE
WITHIN THE CIRCLE FOR THE NOSE.

2

USING THE GUIDE SHAPES, SKETCH A
ROUGH OUTLINE FOR THE MOLE. DRAW A
HEART-SHAPED SNOUT AT THE END OF THE
NOSE AND ADD FIVE CLAWS TO EACH PAW.

3

START SHADING WITH A SOFT PENCIL TO
DEFINE THE SHAPE OF THE HEAD. ADD A FEW
PRICKLY WHISKERS TO THE SNOUT AND
DOTS TO SHOW THE EYE PLACEMENT.

The common mole uses its large, hairless, spade-shaped front feet for digging.

5

USE PAINTS OR PENCILS TO GIVE THE MOLE A GLOSSY BROWN COAT, AND A SHINY PINK NOSE AND PAWS. THEN ADD FINISHING TOUCHES SUCH AS MUD AND GRASS.

The mole's diet consists mostly of earthworms and other soil life. Try adding a few to your drawing!

4

ADD FINAL DETAILS TO YOUR DRAWING BEFORE COLORING, INCLUDING FURTHER DEFINING THE BODY AND CLAWS, AND SKETCHING THE SOIL.

PARAKEET

1 DRAW A CIRCLE FOR EACH PARAKEET'S HEAD AND A SQUASHED OVAL FOR EACH BODY. ADD ROUGH LINES FOR THE TAILS.

2 JOIN EACH HEAD TO ITS BODY WITH LINES, SKETCH IN WINGS, AND GIVE EACH PARAKEET LEGS, FEET, AN EYE, AND A BEAK.

3 USING A HARD PENCIL, FIRM UP THE BEAKS AND EYES. SPEND TIME WORKING ON THE FEATHERS, LEGS, AND TAIL.

4 USE BRIGHT WATERCOLORS FOR THE PARAKEETS' BODIES AND THEN ADD DETAILS WITH COLORED PENCILS.

Parakeets have between 2,000 and 3,000 feathers!

Male parakeets get along well together; they serenade each other.

When drawing feathers, start with a basic outline and add plenty of strokes.

ELEPHANT

AFRICAN ELEPHANTS HAVE LARGE, TRIANGULAR EARS, WHILE ASIAN
ELEPHANTS HAVE SMALLER, ROUNDED EARS. THIS ONE IS AFRICAN!

1

DRAW FIVE ROUGH CIRCLES FOR THE HEAD,
EARS, BODY, AND BASE OF THE TRUNK. THEN
ADD TWO SMALL CIRCLES FOR EYES.

2

NEXT, ADD GUIDELINES FOR THE TRUNK AND
LEGS. THEN SKETCH DASHED LINES FOR THE
BASIC POSITIONS OF THE THREE VISIBLE FEET.

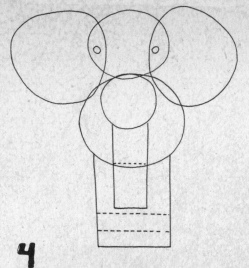

3

USE A SOFT PENCIL TO SKETCH IN THE BASIC
OUTLINE. ADD WAVY LINES FOR THE OUTSIDE
OF THE EARS AND TRUNK, AND TWO TUSKS.

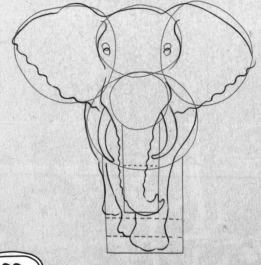

4

WORK UP THE EYES, THEN DRAW CURVED
LINES DOWN THE TRUNK. DO THE SAME FOR
THE KNEES, WHICH ARE LOW ON AN ELEPHANT.

5

USE A BLUE-GRAY WATERCOLOR
WASH. ADD PINK TO THE TIPS OF
THE EARS. PAINT THE TUSKS WHITE.
DRAW THE FINAL LINE WITH A DEEP
BLUE PENCIL.

The large surface area of
an elephant's ears helps
to keep it cool under the
harsh African sun.

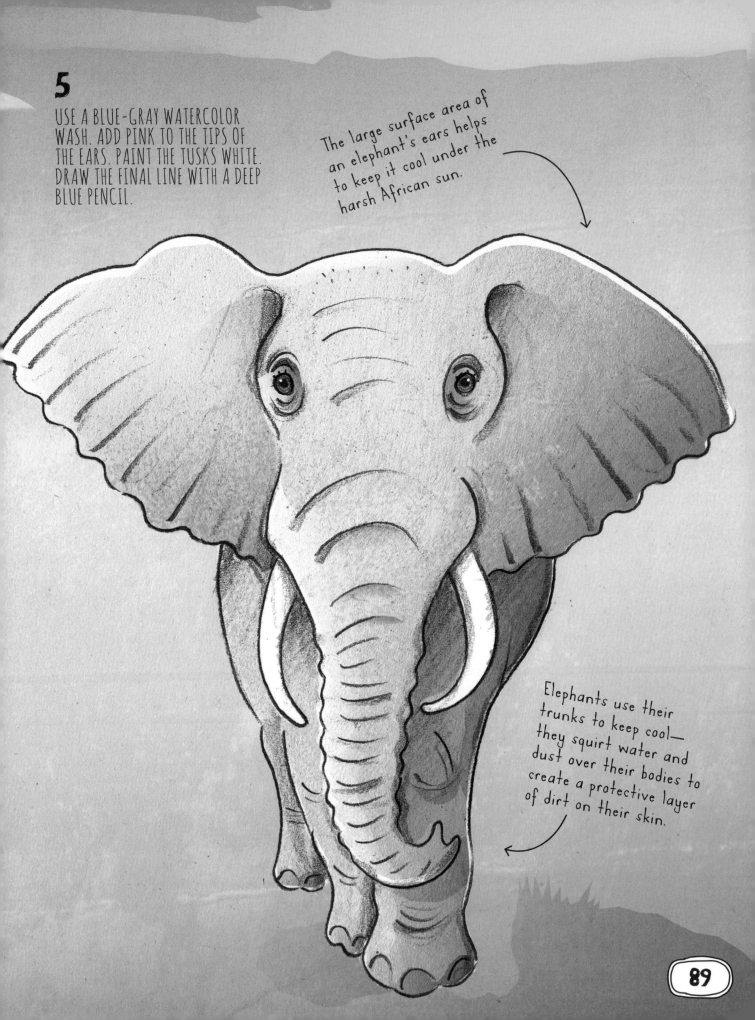

Elephants use their
trunks to keep cool—
they squirt water and
dust over their bodies to
create a protective layer
of dirt on their skin.

FOX

A VIXEN MOTHER STAYS WITH HER CUBS IN THEIR EARTH UNTIL THEY ARE TWO WEEKS OLD. THE DOG FATHER BRINGS THEM FOOD!

1

DRAW THREE OVERLAPPING OVALS. THE LARGER ONE WILL BE THE FOX'S BODY AND THE TWO SMALLER OVALS WILL BE ITS HEAD AND HIND LEG.

2

ADD ANOTHER LARGE OVAL FOR THE TAIL. ADD THREE SMALL OVALS FOR FEET. ADD TRIANGLES TO FORM THE EARS AND POINTED NOSE.

3

USE A SOFT PENCIL TO CREATE THE OUTLINE, WORKING UP THE LEGS, BODY, AND TAIL. SKETCH ROUGH PLACEMENT OF THE EYES AND NOSE.

1

DRAW A SQUASHED CIRCLE FOR THE CUB'S HEAD, AN EGG SHAPE FOR ITS BODY, AND AN OVAL FOR THE HIND LEG.

2

ADD TRIANGLES FOR EARS, A LONG SAUSAGE SHAPE FOR ITS TAIL, AND SMALL OVALS FOR ITS FEET AND HIND LEG.

3

FILL IN THE OUTLINE OF THE FOX CUB, THEN SKETCH IN THE EYES, NOSE, CLAWS, AND A FEW WHISKERS.

4

ADD A JAGGED LINE TO SHOW THE TIP OF THE TAIL. FINALLY, SKETCH IN DETAILS OF THE EARS, EYES, AND TOES, AND ADD A COUPLE OF WHISKERS.

Compared to other fox species, the red fox is large and can adapt quickly to new environments.

COLOR!

ADD LOTS OF FUR TEXTURE TO BOTH THE RED FOX AND CUBS. USE RED, ORANGE, AND BROWN PENCILS TO GIVE THE FUR LOTS OF HIGHLIGHTS.

HONEYBEE

1 SKETCH OUT A HORIZONTAL SAUSAGE SHAPE FOR THE BEE'S ABDOMEN, A SQUASHED CIRCLE FOR THE THORAX, AND A SMALL OVAL FOR THE HEAD.

2 DRAW TWO LARGE ALMOND SHAPES FOR THE BEE'S WINGS. SKETCH A COUPLE OF ANTENNAE ON ITS HEAD AND A CURVED SECTION TO ITS MOUTH.

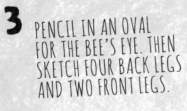

3 PENCIL IN AN OVAL FOR THE BEE'S EYE. THEN SKETCH FOUR BACK LEGS AND TWO FRONT LEGS.

4 ADD STRIPES WITH VERTICAL PENCIL LINES AND HORIZONTAL STROKES. USE A SOFT PENCIL TO GIVE YOUR BEE FLUFFY HAIR.

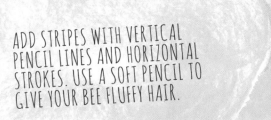

Bees make honey by taking nectar from flowers and digesting it in their mouths!

5 COLOR USING A MIXTURE OF BROWN, ORANGE, AND YELLOW PENCILS ON THE FUR, AND BLACK ON THE LEGS, EYE, AND ANTENNAE. ADD A SPLASH OF WHITE FOR HIGHLIGHTS TO COMPLETE THE DRAWING.

WILD HORSE

1 DRAW TWO CIRCLES FOR THE BODY AND A SQUASHED OVAL FOR THE HEAD. CONNECT WITH LINES. ADD LINES FOR THE LEGS AND CIRCLES FOR JOINTS AND FEET.

2 USING THE GUIDE SHAPES, CREATE A ROUGH OUTLINE. ADD A DOT FOR AN EYE, TWO EARS, AND THE BEGINNINGS OF THE NOSE AND MOUTH.

Wild horses come in a variety of colors, such as gray, white, and black, but "roan" brown, half are around (reddish-brown).

Draw the horse's long tail blowing in the wind!

3

REFINE THE SHAPE
OF THE NOSE AND
ADD LINES TO
SHOW MUSCULAR
DEFINITION. BEGIN
TO ROUGHLY SHAPE THE
MANE AND TAIL.

4

ADD A LIGHT BROWN
WATERCOLOR WASH, SOME FLUFFY
LINES AROUND THE HOOVES,
AND FINALIZE THE DETAIL OF THE
HORSE'S FACE. THEN FINISH WITH
WARM BROWN TONES AND BLACK
TO ADD MUSCLE DEFINITION.

ORANGUTAN

1

DRAW AN OVAL FOR THE BODY, A CIRCLE FOR THE FACE, A CURVE FOR THE FOREHEAD, AND A CIRCLE FOR THE EAR. ADD SAUSAGE-SHAPED LEGS AND ARMS.

2

PENCIL IN THE HANDS AND FEET WITH FINGERS AND TOES. USING A SOFT PENCIL, SKETCH AROUND THE SHAPES TO FORM THE OVERALL OUTLINE.

3

ADD DETAIL TO THE FACE, FEET, AND HANDS. SKETCH HAIR LINES ALL OVER. ADD SMALL LINES FOR ITS NOSTRILS AND ROUNDED M-SHAPED EYEBROWS.

4
USING THE SOFT PENCIL AGAIN, BUILD UP THE LAYERS OF HAIR EVEN FURTHER TO GIVE IT PLENTY OF DEPTH AND TEXTURE.

5
USING PENCILS, PAINT, OR CRAYONS, COVER THE BODY WITH REDDISH-ORANGE HAIR. USE A GRAY WASH ON THE FACE, HANDS, AND FEET.

Orangutans move by swinging from one branch to another. This is called brachiating!

MOUNTAIN GOAT

MOUNTAIN GOATS ONLY INHABIT THE ROCKY MOUNTAINS OF NORTH AMERICA—DRAW YOURS IN A MOUNTAIN SETTING, WITH BOULDERS AND STONES!

Female mountain goats, or nannies, spend most of the year in herds with the young goats, or kids.

2

SKETCH AROUND THE OVALS TO FORM THE OVERALL OUTLINE. ADD AN EAR, EYE, NOSE, MOUTH, AND HOOVES.

3

USING THE SIDE OF A SOFT PENCIL, SKETCH ALL OVER THE BODY TO SHOW THE TEXTURE OF THE WOOL.

1

DRAW TWO OVALS—ONE FOR THE HEAD, ONE FOR THE BODY. ADD SAUSAGE-SHAPED HORNS AND LEGS.

Mountain goats have a thick wool coat that keeps them warm at high elevations.

4

USE LIGHT BROWN AND GRAY PENCILS TO COLOR. ADD TEXTURE TO THE WOOL WITH A LIGHT BROWN PENCIL AND USE BLACK FOR THE EYES, NOSE, MOUTH, AND HOOVES.

REPTILE SCALES

REPTILE SKIN IS MADE UP OF THOUSANDS OF SCALES. HERE ARE A FEW DIFFERENT CLOSE-UPS TO SHOW YOU THE KIND OF DETAILS YOU CAN ADD TO YOUR DRAWINGS!

CROCODILE

Start with lines of rough diamond shapes, then add ovals in the middle of each scale.

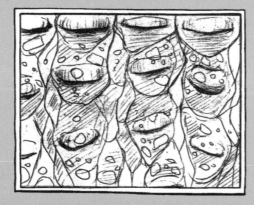
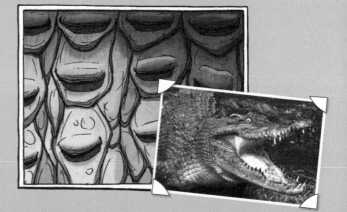

SEA TURTLE

Draw large irregular pentagon shapes that slot into one another.

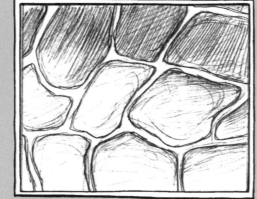
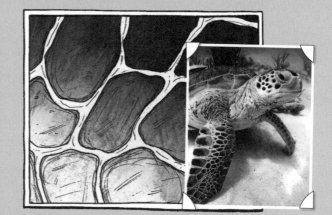

GILA MONSTER

Start with irregular splodges, then add regular circular bumps.

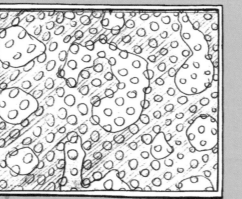
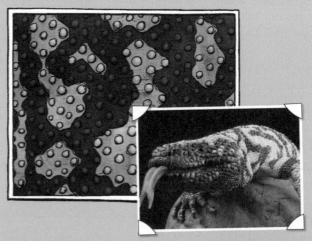

GREEN IGUANA

Draw vertical lines of rough rectangles, one below the other.

CHAMELEON

Draw wavy horizontal lines, then add different-sized circles within the lines.

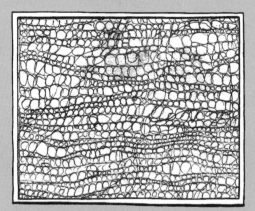

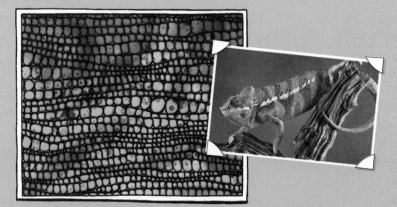

EMERALD TREE BOA

Add diamond-shaped scales one line at a time.

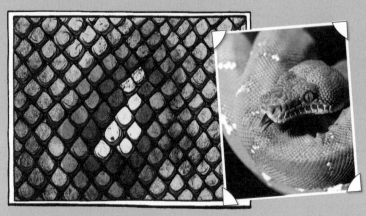

PIGLET

1 START WITH BASIC SHAPES FOR EACH PIGLET. DRAW A SQUASHED CIRCLE FOR EACH BODY AND A FULL CIRCLE FOR EACH HEAD. SKETCH ROUGH LINES FOR THEIR LEGS.

2 NEXT, WORK ON THE OUTLINE OF EACH PIGLET. ADD POINTED EARS TO THEIR HEADS AND CYLINDRICAL SNOUTS. THEN BUILD UP THEIR LEGS.

3 FIRM UP THE FINAL OUTLINE OF EACH PIGLET AND ADD GUIDELINES FOR THE EYES. WITH THOSE IN PLACE, ADD DOTS FOR EACH EYE, SNOUT, AND MOUTH WITH A HARD PENCIL.

4 ADD PLENTY OF DETAIL TO EACH PIGLET, FROM TUFTS OF HAIR AND CURLY TAILS TO EARS AND TROTTERS. REMEMBER TO MAKE EACH PIGLET LOOK SCRUFFY AND PLAYFUL.

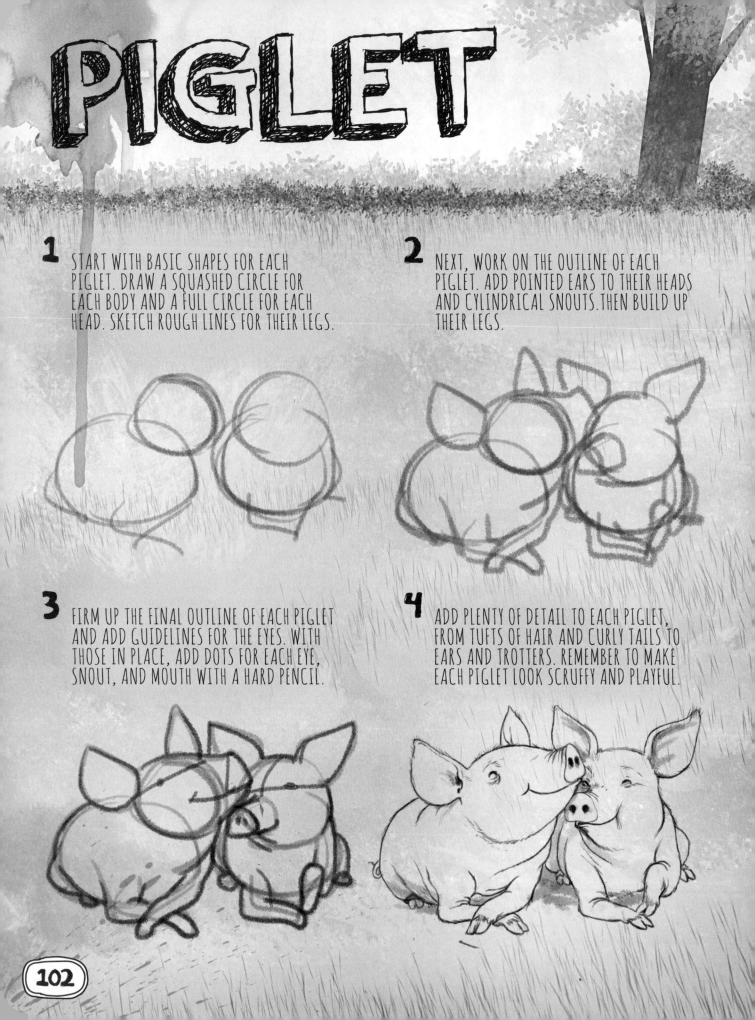

YOUNG PIGLETS ARE VERY SOCIABLE. THEY OFTEN HUDDLE TOGETHER FOR WARMTH AND COMFORT. LEARN TO DRAW TWO CUDDLED UP TOGETHER!

Pigs eat all kinds of things, including vegetables, fruit, and even insects.

5 TO COLOR, USE PINK TONES, WITH BROWN SPLASHES OF MUD ON THEIR TROTTERS AND BELLIES. START WITH A BASE COLOR AND ADD LIGHTS AND DARKS UNTIL YOU'RE HAPPY.

CHEETAH

CHEETAHS ARE THE FASTEST LAND-BASED ANIMALS IN THE WORLD. THEY CAN RUN UP TO 70 MPH TO CATCH ZIGZAGGING PREY!

1

IT'S IMPORTANT TO GET THE SHAPE RIGHT FROM THE START, SO BEGIN WITH TWO BEAN SHAPES FOR THE BODY, AND A CIRCLE FOR THE HEAD.

2

NEXT, ADD THE MUZZLE, THEN THE FIRST HALF OF THE LIMBS AND TAIL. THIS WILL HELP ACHIEVE THE CORRECT PROPORTIONS AND POSITIONING.

4

USING THE GUIDE SHAPES, DRAW A CLEAN AND FLUID LINE FOR THE CHEETAH'S BODY SHAPE. FACIAL FEATURES CAN ALSO BE DEFINED NOW.

5

ADD SPOTS ON THE FUR—CREATE CIRCLES AND SHADE THEM IN WITH A SOFT PENCIL. ALSO ADD A STRIPED TIP AT THE TOP OF THE TAIL.

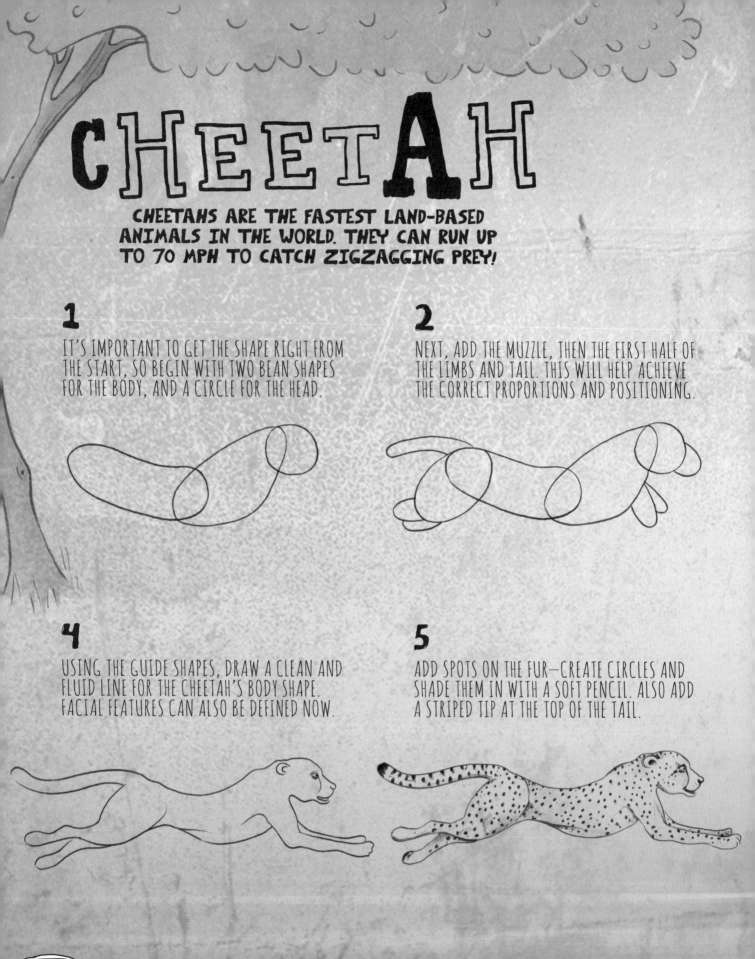

3

NOW ADD THE SECOND HALF OF THE LIMBS. THEN SKETCH IN A ROUGH EYE, EAR, AND NOSE. AT THIS POINT, THE BASIC SHAPE IS COMPLETE.

Now try drawing a running cheetah with all four legs angled into the center of its body!

6

COLOR THE FUR WITH BROWN, ORANGE, AND YELLOW PENCILS. USE A SHARP BLACK PENCIL FOR THE FACE AND SOME SPOTS.

Add subtle horizontal motion lines to give your drawing a real sense of movement!

YELLOW-SPOTTED SALAMANDER

SALAMANDERS ARE AMPHIBIANS THAT LOOK LIKE LIZARDS, BUT THEY LACK SCALES.

1

DRAW A SQUASHED OVAL FOR THE BODY AND A CIRCLE FOR THE HEAD. ADD SMALLER CIRCLES FOR THE LEGS AND A CURVED LINE FOR THE TAIL.

2

SKETCH AROUND THE SHAPES TO FORM THE OUTLINE. DRAW TWO CIRCLES FOR EYES, A CURVED LINE FOR THE SPINE, AND TOES ON EACH FOOT.

3

ADD MORE DETAIL TO THE BODY, WITH HORIZONTAL LINES ON THE TAIL AND ROUND SPOTS ON THE BACK. SKETCH THE EYELIDS AND NOSTRILS.

4

PAINT THE SPOTS YELLOW AND THE BODY BLACK. ADD HIGHLIGHTS WITH GRAY PENCILS TO MAKE THE SKIN LOOK SLICK AND SHINY.

KAISER'S SPOTTED NEWT

A NEWT IS A KIND OF SALAMANDER. ITS SKIN IS NOT AS SMOOTH AS THAT OF OTHER SALAMANDERS.

1

DRAW SEVEN SQUASHED OVALS OF VARYING SIZES FOR THE HEAD, BODY, LEGS, AND TAIL.

2

USING THE GUIDE SHAPES, WORK UP THE OUTLINE AND ADD THE TAIL AND TWO EYES.

3

NOW DRAW A CURVED LINE FOR THE SPINE. THEN ROUGHLY MARK OUT THE SKIN PATTERN.

4

PAINT THE LEGS, FACE, AND SPINE WITH ORANGEY RED. USE A CREAMY YELLOW ON THE SPOTS AND BLACK ON THE PATTERN AND EYE.

PLATYPUS

1

USE A SOFT PENCIL TO SKETCH A LONG OVAL FOR THE BODY AND SQUASHED OVALS AT EACH END FOR THE BEAK AND TAIL.

Although the platypus is a mammal, it has a beak like a bird!

3

HALFWAY UP THE BODY, PLACE ANOTHER WEBBED FOOT. DRAW A LINE ON THE BEAK AND A SMALL BEADY EYE ON THE FACE.

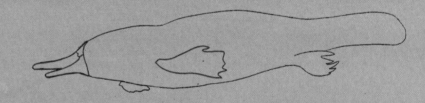

THIS STRANGE-LOOKING ANIMAL IS NATIVE TO AUSTRALIA AND IS ONE OF ONLY A FEW MAMMALS TO LAY EGGS!

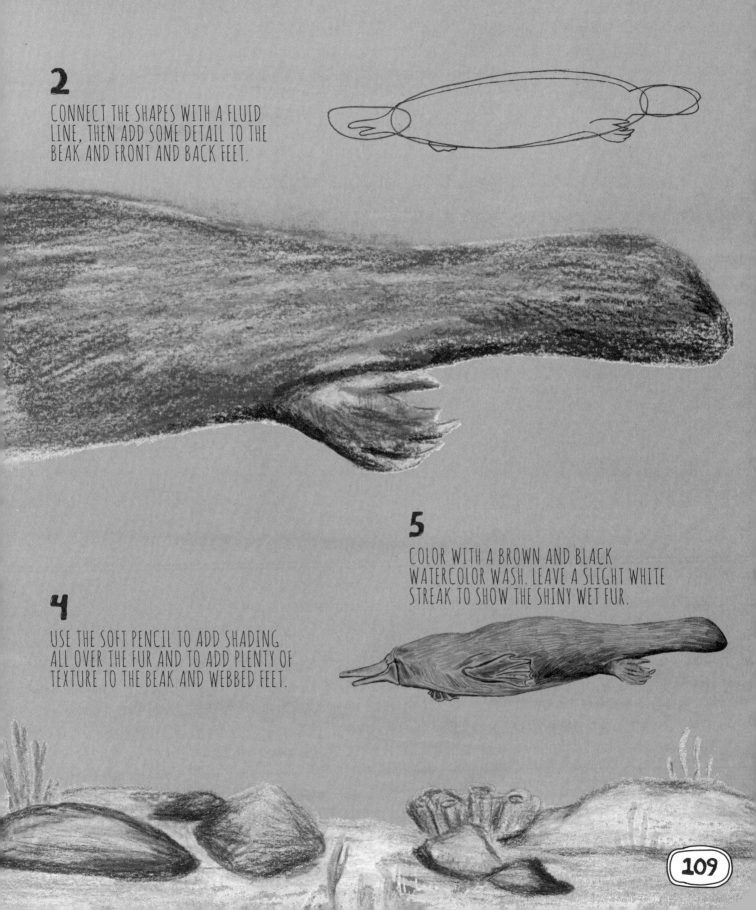

2

CONNECT THE SHAPES WITH A FLUID LINE, THEN ADD SOME DETAIL TO THE BEAK AND FRONT AND BACK FEET.

5

COLOR WITH A BROWN AND BLACK WATERCOLOR WASH. LEAVE A SLIGHT WHITE STREAK TO SHOW THE SHINY WET FUR.

4

USE THE SOFT PENCIL TO ADD SHADING ALL OVER THE FUR AND TO ADD PLENTY OF TEXTURE TO THE BEAK AND WEBBED FEET.

KING COBRA

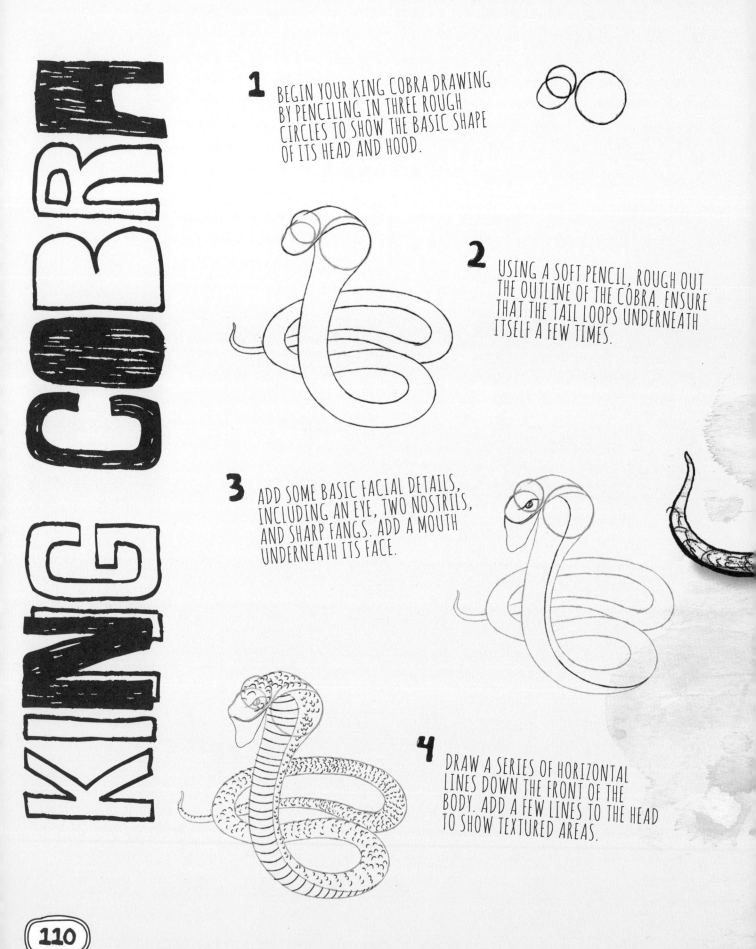

1 BEGIN YOUR KING COBRA DRAWING BY PENCILING IN THREE ROUGH CIRCLES TO SHOW THE BASIC SHAPE OF ITS HEAD AND HOOD.

2 USING A SOFT PENCIL, ROUGH OUT THE OUTLINE OF THE COBRA. ENSURE THAT THE TAIL LOOPS UNDERNEATH ITSELF A FEW TIMES.

3 ADD SOME BASIC FACIAL DETAILS, INCLUDING AN EYE, TWO NOSTRILS, AND SHARP FANGS. ADD A MOUTH UNDERNEATH ITS FACE.

4 DRAW A SERIES OF HORIZONTAL LINES DOWN THE FRONT OF THE BODY. ADD A FEW LINES TO THE HEAD TO SHOW TEXTURED AREAS.

5 PAINT WITH BROWNS, ORANGES, AND YELLOWS. ADD A TOUCH OF WHITE FOR HIGHLIGHTS TO ITS BODY, EYE, AND POINTED FANGS.

When threatened or angry, king cobras rise up, raise their hoods, and prepare to strike!

King cobras are the largest venomous snakes in the world. Try to make yours long and slithery!

111

MOOSE

1

BEGIN WITH AN ANGLED OVAL FOR THE FACE AND TWO CURVED LINES FOR THE BODY. ADD BASIC SAUSAGE SHAPES FOR THE ANTLERS AND EARS.

2

ADD IN DETAIL TO THE FACE WITH TWO EYES, NOSTRILS, AND INSIDE THE EARS. WORK UP THE ANTLERS, MAKING THEM LARGE AND IMPRESSIVE.

3

USING A SOFT PENCIL, BEGIN TO ADD TEXTURE TO THE MOOSE'S FUR. SKETCH A LITTLE MORE DETAIL TO THE FACE AND BODY UNTIL YOU'RE HAPPY.

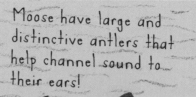

Moose have large and distinctive antlers that help channel sound to their ears!

These large animals need to eat a lot of food. They graze on about 45 lb of plants a day. Add plants to your drawing!

4

COLOR WITH A BROWN WATERCOLOR WASH. USE BROWN PENCILS TO ADD TEXTURE TO THE MOOSE'S FUR AND ANTLERS.

DOLPHIN

BOTTLENOSE DOLPHINS ARE USUALLY FOUND IN TROPICAL WATERS, SO DRAW A SUNNY SCENE TO PLACE THEM IN THEIR NATURAL HABITAT!

1

DRAW A CIRCLE FOR THE HEAD AND A SMALL CIRCLE FOR THE NOSE. SKETCH A CURVED U-SHAPED LINE FOR THE BODY. ADD TWO TRIANGLES FOR THE TAIL.

2

NEXT, START TO FIRM UP THE OVERALL SHAPE OF THE DOLPHIN. ADD TWO SIDE FINS AND A SLIGHTLY LARGER TRIANGULAR FIN ON TOP OF ITS BODY.

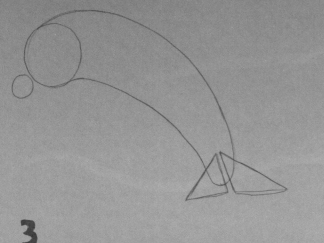

3

WITH A SOFT PENCIL, GO AROUND THE SHAPES TO CREATE THE OUTLINE. TURN THE SHARP-EDGED SHAPES INTO SMOOTHER CURVED SHAPES.

4

BEGIN TO ADD DETAIL TO YOUR DRAWING—ADD A CURVED MOUTH, AN EYE, AND SOME SHADING AROUND THE FINS AND TAIL.

Dolphins can jump up to
20 ft out of the water.
Place yours in midair,
with splashes below!

5

COLOR USING GRAY AND BLUE WATERCOLORS.
USE WHITE FOR THE EYE AND FOR HIGHLIGHTS
ALL OVER, GIVING IT A SLEEK, WET LOOK.

TOUCAN

The toco toucan's bright orange beak is 8 in long—a third of the bird's total length!

1

USE SQUASHED OVAL SHAPES FOR THE BODY, HEAD AND TAIL. CONNECT THE HEAD, AND BODY WITH TWO LINES FOR THE NECK. ADD SMALL CIRCLES FOR THE FEET.

2

DRAW A CIRCLE FOR THE EYE AND SKETCH TWO DIVIDING LINES ON THE BEAK. ADD A TEARDROP SHAPE FOR THE WING AND SMALL CURVED TOES TO THE FEET.

3

CONNECT THE SHAPES WITH A FLUID OUTLINE. ADD INDIVIDUAL FEATHERS TO THE TAIL AND A LINE AROUND THE NECK TO SHOW THE WHITE AREA.

4

LIGHTLY SHADE THE HEAD AND BODY, LEAVING A WHITE PATCH AROUND THE FACE AND NECK. ADD FEATHERS TO THE WING.

5

PAINT THE BODY BLACK AND ADD BLUE
HIGHLIGHTS WITH A PENCIL. USE BRIGHT
ORANGE AND YELLOW FOR THE BEAK, WITH
A LITTLE BLUE AROUND THE EYE.

BEAVER

1

START WITH SIMPLE SHAPES—PENCIL A CIRCLE FOR THE HEAD, A U-SHAPED LINE FOR THE BODY, AND A CURVED LINE FOR THE TAIL.

2

FIRM UP THE OUTLINE AND ADD GUIDELINES TO THE FACE. DRAW A CIRCLE FOR THE SNOUT, THEN PENCIL IN THE EYES, EARS, AND NOSTRILS.

1

FOR THIS VERSION, DRAW A CIRCLE FOR A HEAD AND ADD BASIC GUIDELINES FOR THE SPINE, TAIL, AND LEGS.

2

USING THE GUIDE SHAPES AND LINES, WORK UP THE BODY, LEGS, TAIL, AND SNOUT. ADD ROUGH CLAWS TO THE HANDS.

3

WITH A SOFT PENCIL, BREAK UP THE OUTLINE TO SHOW FUR. ADD DETAIL TO THE FACE AND HANDS, AND START SHADING.

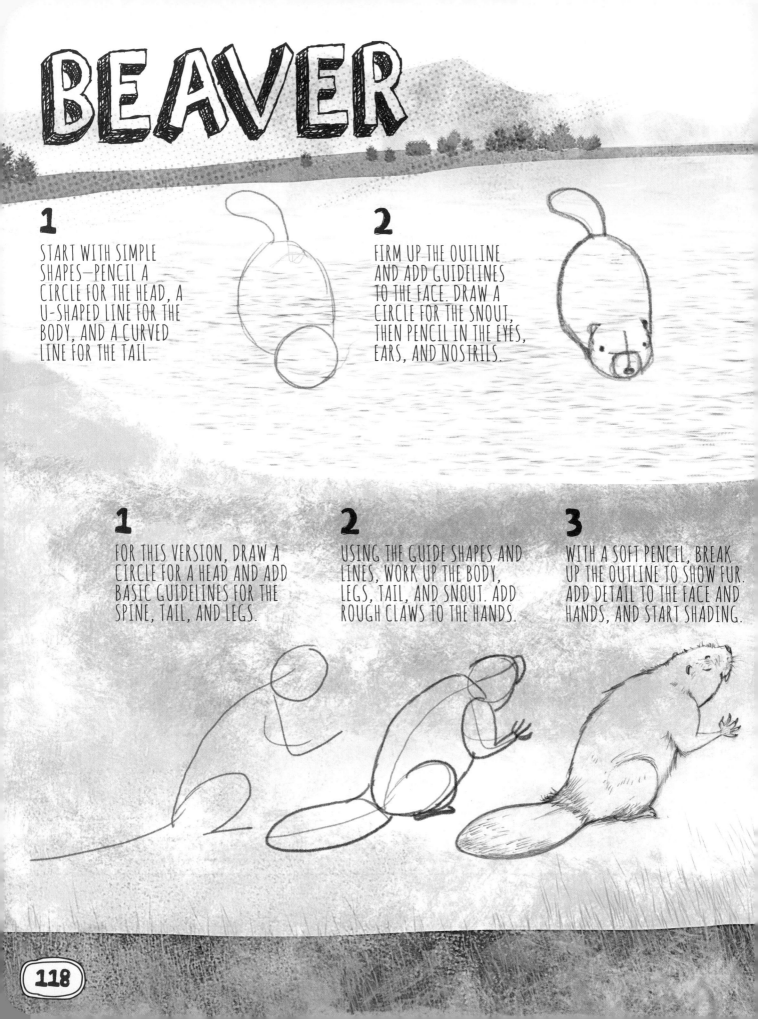

3

DRAW LINES TO CREATE TEXTURE ON THE FUR. DRAW TWO BUCK TEETH HOLDING A TWIG. SKETCH WATER LINES AROUND THE BEAVER.

4

COLOR WITH BROWN, ORANGE, AND GRAY PENCILS. ADD A TOUCH OF YELLOW AROUND THE FACE AND GO OVER THE DETAILS IN BLACK.

4

COLOR WITH BROWN AND GRAY PENCILS. ADD A LITTLE ORANGE AND WHITE TO THE FUR AND WHITE TO THE TAIL.

Beavers use their large, strong teeth to gnaw on wood. Try adding a fallen tree and sawdust to your drawing!

Beavers have large paddle-shaped tails and webbed feet to help them swim!

119

OSTRICH

An ostrich has the largest eye of any land animal, at 2 in across!

1

DRAW A CIRCULAR HEAD WITH AN OVAL MOUTH. DRAW TWO CIRCLES FOR EYES AND THE ROUGH INSIDE OF THE MOUTH.

2

ADD EYELASHES AND MOUTH DETAILS. SKETCH AROUND THE HEAD SHAPE, WITH QUICK FLICK LINES FOR THE FEATHERS.

3

USE A MIX OF GRAY, BLACK, AND WHITE PENCILS TO COLOR THE FEATHERS, WITH RED AND ORANGE FOR THE MOUTH.

1

DRAW SQUASHED CIRCLES FOR THE HEAD, BODY, AND TAIL. ADD A LONG NECK AND SAUSAGE SHAPES FOR LEGS.

2

NEXT, DEFINE THE OVERALL OUTLINE OF THE OSTRICH, BREAKING THE LINE AT THE TAIL AND TOP OF THE HEAD.

3

PAINT THE FEATHERS GRAY AND BLACK AND THE LEGS WHITE. THEN ADD GRAY HIGHLIGHTS ON BOTH.

Ostriches are fast runners and can sprint at up to 40 mph!

LLAMA

Draw a squashed oval body, circular head, and guidelines for the legs. Work up the outline and facial details. Color with yellow and brown washes. Add gray highlights.

Llama wool is soft, oil-free, and lightweight, so it is great for all kinds of things!

WOOLLY ANIMALS

ALPACA

Sketch a squashed oval head, U-shaped body, and triangular ears. Refine the outline and facial details. Color with a white and brown wash. Then use orange and gray pencils to add highlights.

Alpaca fleece is soft and fine. It is similar to sheep's wool, but it is warmer and lighter.

ANGORA GOAT

Pencil a rough square for the body, with a circle for a head. Draw the overall outline and add details. Color with light brown, yellow, and gray pencils.

The wool, or fleece, taken from Angora goats is called "mohair." It makes a silklike yarn.

SHEEP

Draw a large circle for the body and two circles for the head. Add the outline and details. Use a light yellow wash, then add texture with brown and gray pencils.

The fleece of a sheep is quite greasy—it is full of a substance called lanolin (wool wax).

ARMADILLO

1

BEGIN BY DRAWING A LARGE SQUASHED OVAL FOR THE BODY, A SMALL TAPERED HEAD, LONG TRIANGULAR TAIL, AND FOUR OVAL FEET.

2

ADD LEAF-SHAPED EARS AND A SMALL ROUND EYE. DRAW STRIPED BANDS ON THE BODY AND TAIL, THEN ADD SOME DETAIL TO THE FEET AND HEAD.

1

START WITH A LARGE OVAL FOR THE ARMADILLO'S BODY, THEN ADD A TAPERED HEAD AND FOUR SMALL SQUASHED OVALS FOR THE LEGS.

2

DRAW BASIC LINES ON THE BODY TO SHOW ITS ARMOR PATTERN. ADD CLAWS, EARS, AN EYE, AND A WAVY HORIZONTAL LINE ON ITS HEAD.

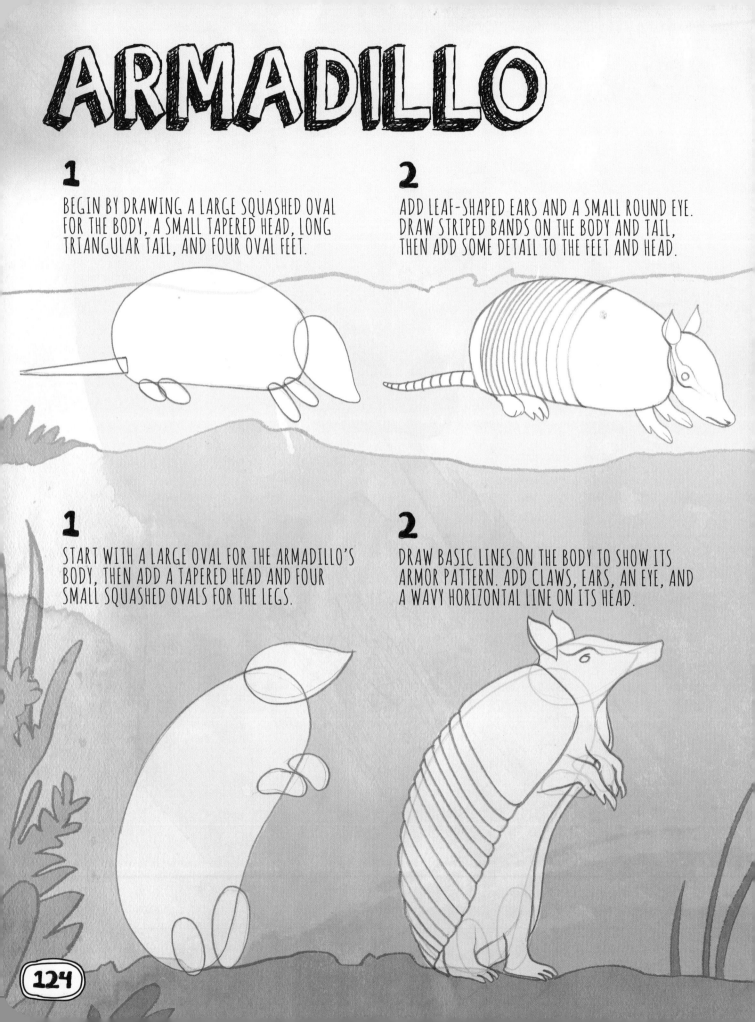

3

COLOR USING BROWN WATERCOLORS.
USE A HARD, DARK BROWN PENCIL TO
ADD THE SCALES IN THE BANDS AND
PATTERN ON THE HEAD.

Unlike other armadillos,
this nine-banded
armadillo isn't able to roll
into a ball for protection!

3

FOR THIS VERSION, PAINT THE UNDERSIDE WITH
BROWN WATERCOLORS AND BROWN PENCILS.
USE LIGHTER TONES FOR THE SHELL.

For the armadillo's armor
plating, draw evenly
spaced dark lines with
a hard pencil, then add
rows of fish-scale shapes
side by side.

KOALA

A baby koala is called a joey. They have even softer fur and much smaller ears than adults!

1

SKETCH AN OVAL FOR THE BODY AND A CIRCLE FOR THE HEAD. ADD A BASIC BACK LEG AND ARM. JOIN THE SHAPES AND ADD EARS, EYES, NOSE, AND MOUTH.

2

USING A SOFT PENCIL, BREAK UP THE LINE WITH SOME BASIC SHADING TO SHOW THE FUR TEXTURE. ADD SMALL CLAWS TO THE FOOT AND HAND.

3

COLOR USING GRAY AND LIGHT BROWN PENCILS.
ADD HIGHLIGHTS IN WHITE PAINT USING A STIPPLE
BRUSH. USE A BLACK PENCIL FOR THE EYES, NOSE,
AND CLAWS, AND AROUND THE MOUTH.

Koalas are mostly
nocturnal. They
often sleep in tree
branches for up to
18-20 hours a day!

LABRADOR RETRIEVER

YEARS AGO, LABRADOR RETRIEVERS WERE BRED TO HELP FISHERMEN HAUL NETS, SO THEY LOVE TO SWIM!

1 START WITH A BEAN SHAPE FOR THE BODY. THEN ADD ONE CIRCLE FOR THE HEAD, TWO FOR THE SNOUT, AND ONE FOR THE EYE. DRAW AN OVAL EAR.

2 NEXT, ADD OVALS AND SAUSAGE SHAPES TO MAKE THE LEGS. USE THE BODY TO HELP WITH THEIR POSITION. ADD A LONG, SAUSAGE-SHAPED TAIL.

Labradors have strong, broad tails (which help propel them through water) and slightly webbed toes!

3 SKETCH THE OUTLINE OF THE LABRADOR, BREAKING UP THE LINE WITH STROKES TO CREATE THE LOOK OF FUR. ADD DETAILS AND SHADING.

4 COLOR WITH A LIGHT BROWN WATERCOLOR. USE YELLOW AND WHITE PENCILS TO ADD HIGHLIGHTS, AND PINK FOR THE NOSE.

wEAsEL

THE LONG-TAILED WEASEL'S TAIL MAKES UP AROUND 40 TO 70 PERCENT OF THE ANIMAL'S TOTAL LENGTH!

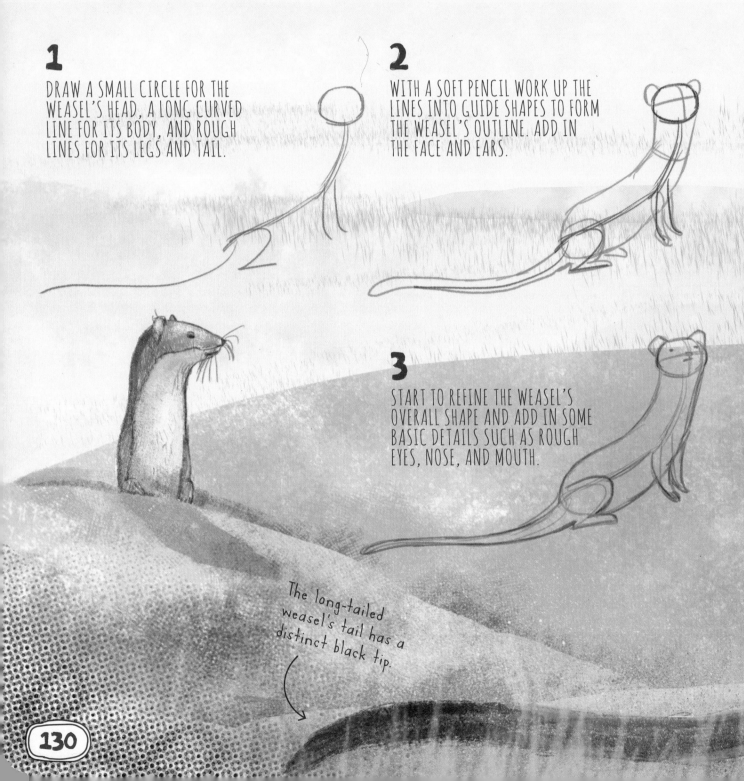

1

DRAW A SMALL CIRCLE FOR THE WEASEL'S HEAD, A LONG CURVED LINE FOR ITS BODY, AND ROUGH LINES FOR ITS LEGS AND TAIL.

2

WITH A SOFT PENCIL WORK UP THE LINES INTO GUIDE SHAPES TO FORM THE WEASEL'S OUTLINE. ADD IN THE FACE AND EARS.

3

START TO REFINE THE WEASEL'S OVERALL SHAPE AND ADD IN SOME BASIC DETAILS SUCH AS ROUGH EYES, NOSE, AND MOUTH.

The long-tailed weasel's tail has a distinct black tip.

4

USING A HARD PENCIL, BEGIN SKETCHING IN A FEW LINES ON THE BODY TO SHOW FUR. ADD IN WHISKERS AND THE INNER EARS.

5

TO COLOR, COMBINE BROWN AND ORANGE PENCILS, WITH BLACK FOR THE EYES AND TAIL TIP. USE SMALL STROKES TO ACHIEVE THE TEXTURE OF THE FUR.

Its small head and long, thin body are perfect for hunting its prey in their own burrows!

TIGER

TIGERS ARE AMBUSH HUNTERS. DRAW YOURS HIDING AMONG THE LEAVES, READY TO JUMP OUT AND ATTACK ITS PREY!

1

DRAW A CIRCLE. ADD A VERTICAL LINE AND TWO HORIZONTAL LINES. DRAW A V-SHAPED LINE TO HELP YOU DRAW TWO EARS. ADD CURVED LINES FOR THE CHIN AND SIDES OF THE FACE.

2

PENCIL A V-SHAPED NOSE AND W-SHAPED SNOUT. DRAW EYES ON THE UPPER LINE, CLOSE TO THE W-SHAPED LINE. NOW ADD A FEW LINES FOR THE TIGER'S BODY.

3

ADD PUPILS AND DRAW WINGED SHAPES AROUND THEM TO START SHOWING THE TIGER'S MARKINGS. USE THE CIRCLE SHAPE TO DEFINE THE EDGES OF THE TIGER'S FACE.

4

DRAW LINES UNDER THE NOSE FOR THE WHISKERS. ADD FUR MARKINGS AROUND THE EDGE OF THE FACE AND A FEW STRIPES TO THE BODY.

5

START TO SHADE IN THE BLACK STRIPES AND WORK UP THE HAIR AROUND THE FACE. NEXT, ADD DOTS ALONG THE LINES ON THE NOSE.

6

FIRST, GIVE THE FACE AN ORANGE WATERCOLOR WASH. THEN USE WHITE TO COLOR THE AREA AROUND THE EYES, EDGES OF FUR, SNOUT, AND CHIN. ADD PINK TO THE NOSE AND GREEN TO THE EYES. USE A WHITE PENCIL TO ADD WHISKERS.

Each tiger's stripes are unique, just like human fingerprints. So don't worry if yours doesn't look exactly like this one!

133

CARIBOU

CARIBOU ARE THE ONLY SPECIES OF DEER WHOSE MALES AND FEMALES BOTH HAVE ANTLERS. THIS ONE IS FROM THE PORCUPINE CARIBOU HERD!

1

START WITH A SMALL SQUASHED OVAL FOR THE HEAD AND A LARGE OVAL FOR THE BODY. ADD BASIC SAUSAGE SHAPES FOR THE FOUR LEGS.

2

USING THE GUIDE SHAPES, DRAW THE OUTLINE OF THE CARIBOU'S BODY AND NECK. SKETCH A SMALL TAIL AND AN EAR.

3

FOR THE CARIBOU'S ANTLERS, PENCIL IN TWO SLIGHTLY OVERLAPPING C-SHAPES TO GET THE SIZE AND LOOK OF THEM JUST RIGHT.

Porcupine caribou migrate over 800 mi every year, from their winter range to summer calving grounds!

4

ADD CURVY BRANCHING SHAPES TO THE ANTLERS. THEN WORK ON THE FACE, ADDING AN EYE, NOSE, AND MOUTH. DRAW THE HOOVES AND FUR.

5

PAINT WITH SHADES OF BROWN. THEN USE A WHITE PENCIL TO ADD LIGHT PATCHES ON THE STOMACH, LEGS, NECK, AND TAIL.

SEA TURTLE

1

DRAW A CIRCLE AND SQUASHED OVAL FOR THE HEAD. ADD A LARGE OVAL FOR THE BODY AND TWO FLATTENED OVALS EITHER SIDE OF IT FOR FINS.

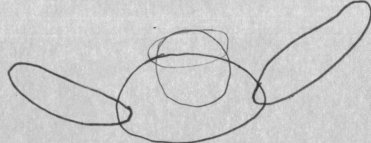

2

SKETCH AROUND THE GUIDE SHAPES TO FORM THE OUTLINE. ADD TWO EYES, NOSTRILS, A MOUTH, AND LINES TO SHOW THE FACE SHAPE.

3

USE A SOFT PENCIL TO SKETCH A ROUGH SKIN PATTERN ON THE FINS AND HEAD, AND START TO ADD SHADING TO THE SHELL.

4

COLOR WITH A YELLOW WATERCOLOR WASH, THEN ADD THE GREEN WATERCOLOR. USE BROWN AND BLACK FOR SHADING.

The green sea turtle is named not for the color of its shell, which is normally brown or olive, but for the greenish color of its skin!

SKIN AND SHELL

The color of the turtle's shell, or carapace, changes over time. The pattern on its shell, head, and fins is made up of lots of different plates called "scutes!"

HUMMINGBIRD

THIS SMALL RUFOUS HUMMINGBIRD BEATS ITS WINGS MORE THAN 200 TIMES A SECOND IN ORDER TO HOVER IN MIDAIR WHILE COLLECTING NECTAR FROM FLOWERS!

Try blurring the wings to create a sense of movement.

1

DRAW A CIRCLE FOR THE HEAD AND AN OVAL FOR THE BODY. ADD IN BASIC LINES FOR THE BIRD'S TAIL, BEAK, AND WINGS.

2

USE A SOFT PENCIL TO DRAW A SMOOTH OUTLINE. ADD A BEAK AND SOME ROUGH FEATHERS TO THE TAIL.

3

DRAW THE ROUGH OUTLINE OF ANOTHER SET OF WINGS BEHIND THE FIRST. ADD THE BIRD'S EYE AND A FEW FEATHER TEXTURES.

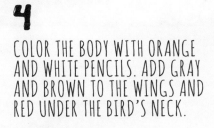

4

COLOR THE BODY WITH ORANGE AND WHITE PENCILS. ADD GRAY AND BROWN TO THE WINGS AND RED UNDER THE BIRD'S NECK.

CHIPMUNK

1

DRAW AN OVAL FOR THE CHIPMUNK'S HEAD, THEN A LARGE OVAL FOR ITS BODY AND SAUSAGE SHAPES FOR ITS HAND, LEG, EAR, AND TAIL.

2

USE A SOFT PENCIL TO FIRM UP THE CHIPMUNK'S OVERALL OUTLINE. ADD IN AN EYE, A NOSE, SOME BASIC EAR DETAIL, AND TOES.

3

NEXT, BEGIN TO SKETCH THE CHIPMUNK'S DISTINCTIVE FUR PATTERN. ADD A FEW SOFT LINES ON THE BACK AND ACROSS THE HEAD.

CHIPMUNKS ARE SMALL MEMBERS OF THE SQUIRREL FAMILY. THIS ONE IS AN EASTERN CHIPMUNK. IT IS LIVELY AND SPEEDY!

4

COLOR YOUR DRAWING WITH A COMBINATION OF GRAY, BROWN, AND ORANGE PENCILS. ADD BLACK ON THE EYE, EAR, AND FUR STRIPES.

Eastern chipmunks have large cheek pouches, which they use to store and transport food!

GOLDEN RETRIEVER

GOLDEN RETRIEVERS LOVE NOTHING MORE THAN CHASING AND FETCHING BALLS, HENCE THE NAME.

1

START WITH GUIDE SHAPES FOR THE HEAD, EARS, AND BODY. THEN ADD GUIDELINES FOR THE HEAD, FRONT LEGS, AND TAIL. SKETCH THREE CIRCLES FOR THE PAWS AND A BALL.

2

USING THE GUIDELINES, SKETCH THE EYES, NOSE, AND MOUTH. THEN WORK UP THE TAIL, LEGS, AND PAWS. USE A SOFT PENCIL TO ADD FUR TEXTURE.

3

COLOR WITH BROWN, ORANGE, AND YELLOW PENCILS. USE BLACK FOR THE EYES, NOSE, MOUTH, AND NAILS. ADD SOME PINK TO THE TONGUE. USE ANY COLOR YOU WANT FOR THE BALL!

Golden retriever puppies have lots of fluffy fur, so use a soft pencil to achieve this effect!

BEAGLE

BEAGLES ARE MUSCULAR, ATHLETIC DOGS. THEY NEED LOTS OF EXERCISE TO KEEP THEM IN SHAPE.

1

START WITH CIRCLES AND OVALS FOR THE HEAD, BODY, AND LEGS. THEN ADD LINES FOR THE MUZZLE, FRONT LEGS, AND TAIL. SKETCH TWO CIRCLES FOR THE PAWS.

2

USING THE GUIDELINES, ADD THE EYES, NOSE, MOUTH, AND EARS. THEN WORK UP THE REST OF THE BODY, INCLUDING THE TAIL, LEGS, AND PAWS. NOW START SHADING.

3

COLOR WITH BROWN PENCILS. ADD A BIT OF BLACK ON THE FUR, NOSE, EYES, AND NAILS. MAKE SURE YOU LEAVE THE UNDERSIDE AND THE TIP OF THE TAIL WHITE.

LION Draw a squashed oval for the head, with a heart-shaped face, small circles for eyes, and a teardrop nose. Build up layers of fur by using black and brown pencils. Add pink to the mouth and orange to the eyes.

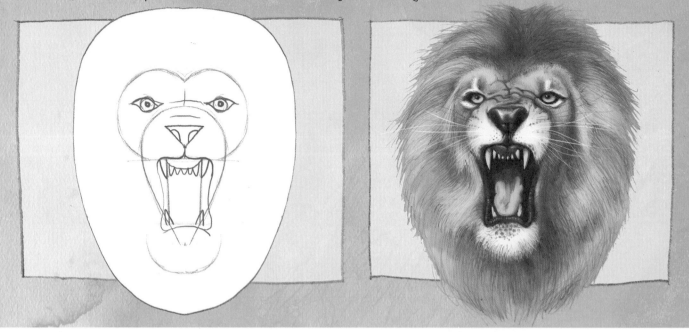

BIG CAT FACES

 **CHEETAH** Sketch squashed triangles for the face and ears. Add vertical lines, eye outlines, and a mouth with a black pencil. Color using brown and orange pencils. Add orange eyes and yellow and white highlights.

144

BLACK PANTHER

Sketch a squashed circle for the head, with triangular ears, small circles for eyes, a U-shaped muzzle, nose, and mouth. Color using black paint and gray pencils. Add yellow eyes.

Black leopards and jaguars are commonly called "black panthers."

TIGERS ARE THE LARGEST OF THE BIG CAT FAMILY, FOLLOWED BY LIONS, JAGUARS, AND LEOPARDS. CHEETAHS AND SNOW LEOPARDS ARE SOMETIMES REFERRED TO AS BIG CATS, TOO.

SNOW LEOPARD

Draw a squashed circle for the head, triangular ears, small circles for eyes and lines for the nose and mouth area. Color with gray, white, and light brown pencils, with a pink nose.

CHAMELEON

CHAMELEONS ARE TREE-LIVING LIZARDS THAT FIRE OUT THEIR LONG TONGUES TO CATCH PREY. THIS ONE IS A VEILED CHAMELEON.

A veiled chameleon's diet consists mostly of insects!

1

DRAW AN OVAL FOR THE BODY, AND AN EGG SHAPE AND A SEMICIRCLE FOR THE HEAD. ADD AN EYE, MOUTH, V-SHAPED LEGS, AND LONG TAIL.

2

SKETCH THE OUTLINE. ADD DETAILS TO THE EYE, MOUTH, AND TOES, AND SPIKES UNDER THE CHIN AND ON THE BACK.

3

NEXT, ADD ROUGH MARKINGS AND SCALES TO THE CHAMELEON'S SKIN. TRY TO MAKE THEM IRREGULAR IN SHAPE AND SIZE.

Chameleons change color depending on their mood and surroundings, so try a few different skin looks!

4

USING A HARD PENCIL, ADD TEXTURE TO THE SCALES AND SKIN. DRAW A LONG TONGUE WITH A FLY ATTACHED TO THE END.

5

USE A GREEN WATERCOLOR WASH FOR THE CHAMELEON'S SKIN. ADD YELLOW TEXTURES AND PINK FOR THE TONGUE.

COW

THIS COW IS LARGE, WITH BLACK AND WHITE MARKINGS. IT IS A TYPE CALLED HOLSTEIN-FRIESIAN, BRED TO PRODUCE MILK TO MAKE DAIRY PRODUCTS.

1

START WITH AN OVAL FOR THE NOSE, THEN ADD TWO U-SHAPED LINES FOR THE HEAD AND BODY. ADD OVALS FOR THE NOSTRIL AND EYE.

2

PENCIL IN CURVED LINES FOR THE TOP OF THE COW'S HEAD, TWO EARS, AND THE OTHER EYE. ADD TWO SAUSAGE SHAPES FOR THE LEGS.

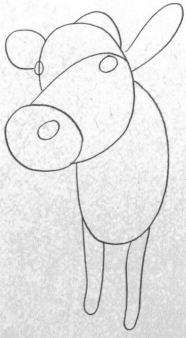

3

NEXT, MARK IN THE AREAS FOR THE COLORED PATCHES ON ITS FACE, BODY, AND LEGS. ADD DETAIL TO THE INSIDE OF THE EARS.

4

USE A SOFT PENCIL TO DEFINE THE OUTLINE, AND ADD SHADING AND EYELASHES. DRAW WAVY LINES FOR THE PATCHES.

5

COLOR WITH A SOFT
BLACK PENCIL,
ADDING DARKER
TONES AROUND THE
EYES AND EARS. USE
A GRAY PENCIL TO
ADD HIGHLIGHTS ON
THE WHITE AREAS.

SAFARI PRINTS

ANIMALS HAVE ALL KINDS OF COAT COLORS AND PATTERNS. TRY YOUR HAND AT THESE DIFFERENT DRAWING TECHNIQUES TO PERFECT YOUR OWN SAFARI PRINTS.

LEOPARD

First draw irregular squashed shapes, then add splodge shapes around the edges of each one. Color with yellow, orange, and brown.

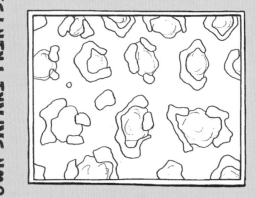

ZEBRA

Create a series of loose horizontal lines using a soft black pencil. Then paint the lines black.

CHEETAH

Mix up C-shapes, jagged ovals, and smaller splodge shapes. Then add slits in the centers. Color with yellow, orange, and brown.

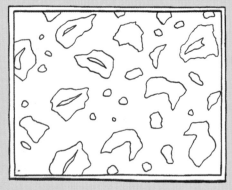

GIRAFFE

Draw interlocking shapes with spaces in between. Try to make each shape a different size. Color each shape reddish-brown, with creamy yellow in between.

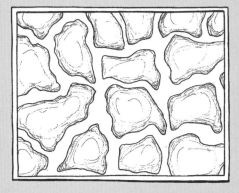 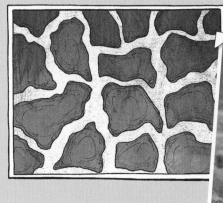 

TIGER

Use a soft pencil to draw two stretched and connected lines for each stripe. First color orange, then add the black.

FUR TEXTURES

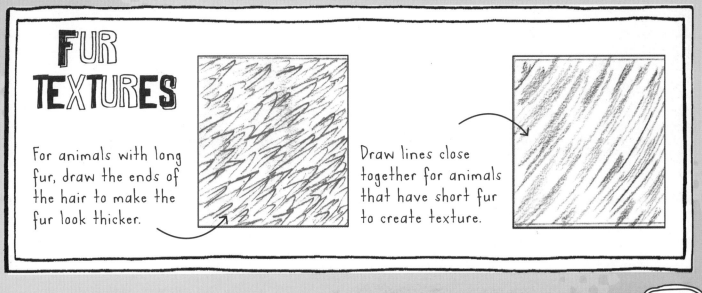

For animals with long fur, draw the ends of the hair to make the fur look thicker.

Draw lines close together for animals that have short fur to create texture.

WOODPECKER

WOODPECKERS CAN PECK UP TO 20 TIMES PER SECOND, OR 800 TO 12,000 TIMES PER DAY! THIS ONE IS A PILEATED WOODPECKER. DRAW IT MID-PECK!

1

DRAW AN OVAL FOR THE BODY, A TRIANGULAR HEAD, BASIC LEGS, AND A LONG, TRIANGULAR TAIL.

2

DEFINE THE OUTLINE WITH A SOFT PENCIL AND ADD SOME DETAIL TO THE BIRD'S LEGS AND FEET.

Woodpeckers build nesting holes in trees all year round.

3

ADD BASIC LINES FOR THE MOUTH, AN EYE, A TUFT OF FEATHERS ON TOP OF THE HEAD, CLAWS, AND TAIL DETAILS.

4

USE A BLACK PENCIL, ADDING BROWN AND WHITE HIGHLIGHTS. ADD RED ON TOP OF ITS HEAD AND UNDER ITS BEAK.

TREE FROG

THIS RAINFOREST-DWELLING AMPHIBIAN IS A RED-EYED TREE FROG. IT FLASHES ITS BULGING RED EYES TO SCARE AWAY PREDATORS!

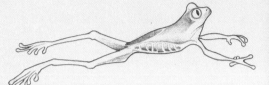

3 ADD ROUNDED PADS TO THE TIPS OF EACH TOE AND A VERTICAL SLIT FOR THE PUPIL. USE A HARD PENCIL TO REFINE THE OUTLINE.

2 CONNECT THE HEAD, BODY, AND LEGS WITH A FLUID OUTLINE AND PENCIL IN LONG-TOED FEET. ADD A CURVED EYE.

1 BEGIN WITH SQUASHED OVALS FOR THE BODY AND HEAD. ADD A CIRCULAR EYE AND SAUSAGE SHAPES FOR THE FOUR LEGS.

3 SKETCH A THIN VERTICAL SLIT FOR A PUPIL AND DARK SHADING AROUND THE EYES. ADD A PATTERN TO THE BODY.

2 ADD LARGE FEET WITH SPLAYED TOES, A SECOND EYE, AND A THIN MOUTH. CONNECT ALL OF THE SHAPES WITH A FLUID OUTLINE.

1 START WITH A LARGE OVAL FOR THE BODY AND HEAD. ADD A LARGE ROUND EYE AND THIN PIPE SHAPES FOR THE SKINNY LEGS.

COLOR!

USE BRIGHT GREEN AND YELLOW PAINT ON THE BODY, WITH A TOUCH OF ELECTRIC BLUE ON THE THIGHS AND STRIPES. COLOR THE FEET ORANGE AND YELLOW, AND THE EYE RED AND BLACK.

The hands and feet are large in comparison to the body, and the long, thin fingers end with large, round pads.

The skin of a tree frog is almost translucent in appearance. Layer shading to achieve this effect.

FLAMINGO

FLAMINGOS LIVE IN GROUPS CALLED FLOCKS OR STANDS RANGING FROM A FEW TO A THOUSAND. THESE TWO ARE GREATER FLAMINGOS!

1

START YOUR DRAWING WITH A SIMPLE OVAL FOR THE FLAMINGO'S BODY AND A SMALLER OVAL FOR ITS HEAD. ADD ROUGH VERTICAL LINES FOR THE LEGS.

2

USE CURVED, FLOWING LINES TO PENCIL IN THE NECK. ADD MORE DETAIL FOR THE FLAMINGO'S LEGS AND A BASIC TRIANGLE SHAPE FOR THE TAIL.

156

3

DRAW THE BEAK POINTING DOWNWARD AND THE LINE FOR THE MOUTH SLIGHTLY OFF-CENTER. ADD THE KNEE JOINTS TO THE LEGS.

4

NEXT, PENCIL IN PLENTY OF DETAIL TO THE FLAMINGO'S FEATHERS AND WINGS, THEN ADD A CURVED LINE TO FORM THE JOINING LINE OF THE BEAK AND AN EYE.

Flamingos spend a lot of time wading in water, searching for food, such as insects, algae, and small fish!

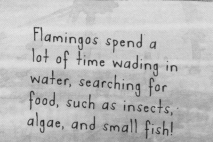

5

COLOR WITH A PINK WATERCOLOR WASH. ADD DEFINITION WITH DARK PINK AND RED PENCILS. USE BLACK FOR THE BEAK TIP AND UNDER THE WING.

157

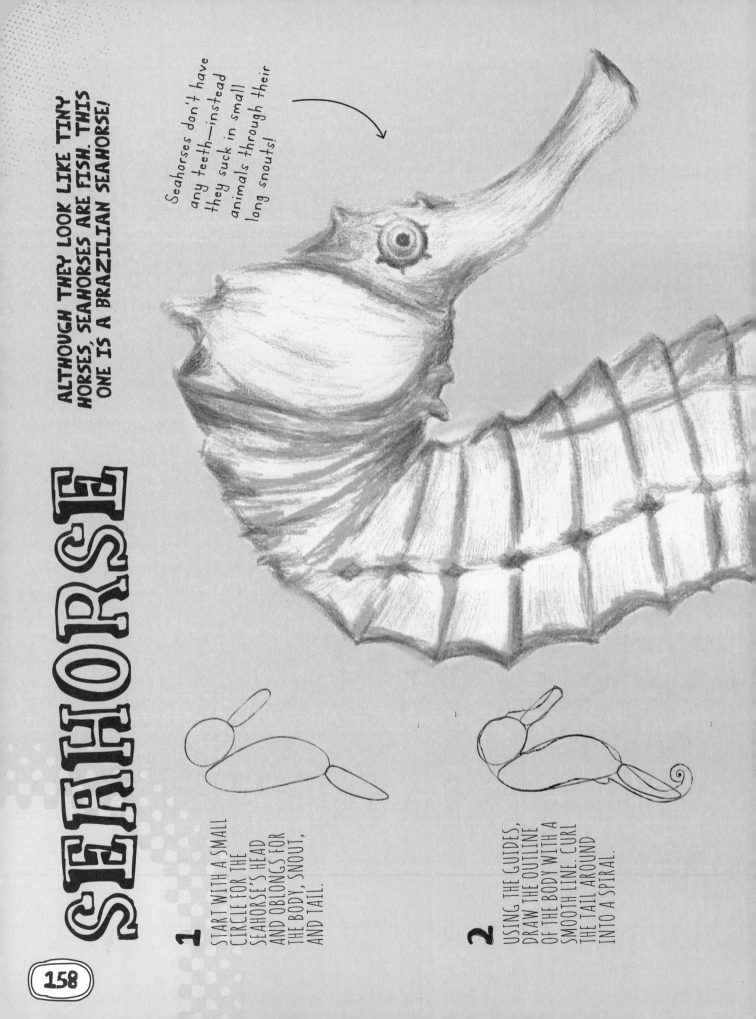

SEAHORSE

ALTHOUGH THEY LOOK LIKE TINY HORSES, SEAHORSES ARE FISH. THIS ONE IS A BRAZILIAN SEAHORSE!

Seahorses don't have any teeth—instead they suck in small animals through their long snouts!

1 START WITH A SMALL CIRCLE FOR THE SEAHORSE'S HEAD AND OBLONGS FOR THE BODY, SNOUT, AND TAIL.

2 USING THE GUIDES, DRAW THE OUTLINE OF THE BODY WITH A SMOOTH LINE. CURL THE TAIL AROUND INTO A SPIRAL.

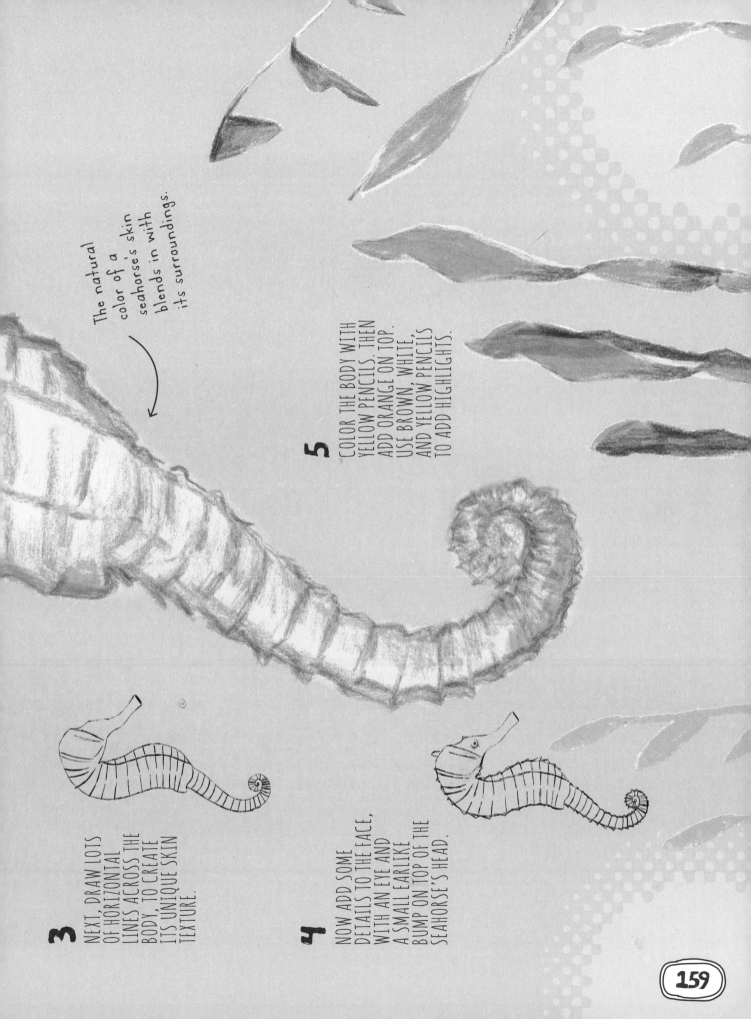

The natural color of a seahorse's skin blends in with its surroundings.

5
COLOR THE BODY WITH YELLOW PENCILS. THEN ADD ORANGE ON TOP. USE BROWN, WHITE, AND YELLOW PENCILS TO ADD HIGHLIGHTS.

3
NEXT, DRAW LOTS OF HORIZONTAL LINES ACROSS THE BODY, TO CREATE ITS UNIQUE SKIN TEXTURE.

4
NOW ADD SOME DETAILS TO THE FACE, WITH AN EYE AND A SMALL EARLIKE BUMP ON TOP OF THE SEAHORSE'S HEAD.

GUINEA PIG

1

DRAW TWO EGG SHAPES AS GUIDES FOR THE HEADS, A CIRCLE AS A GUIDE FOR THE LEFT GUINEA PIG'S BODY, SMALL OVALS FOR THE EARS, AND SEMICIRCLES FOR THE FEET.

2

USING THE GUIDE SHAPES, SKETCH A ROUGH OUTLINE FOR EACH GUINEA PIG AND ERASE UNNECESSARY LINES. DRAW GUIDELINES FOR THE FACES—ONE VERTICAL, FOUR HORIZONTAL.

3

NOW USING THE GUIDELINES, DRAW BASIC EYES, NOSE, MOUTH, AND CHIN. DEFINE THE OUTLINES OF THE GUINEA PIGS, INCLUDING THE EARS, LEGS, AND FEET.

4

SHADE IN THE EYES AND START ROUGHING OUT SOME FUR TEXTURES. A LOT OF THE GUINEA PIG'S SHAPE AND PERSONALITY IS ACHIEVED THROUGH SHADING.

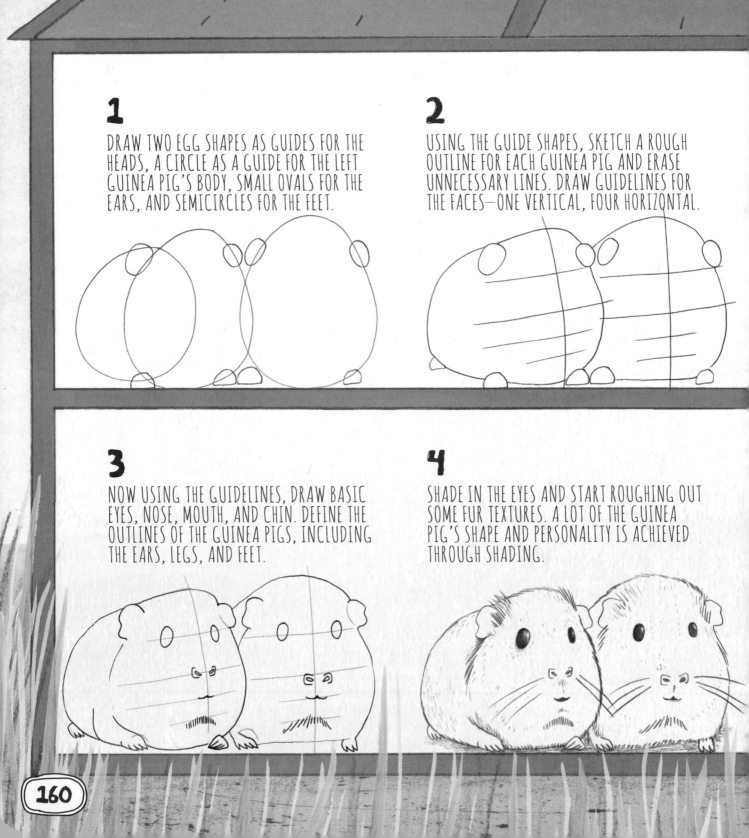

5

GIVE THE GUINEA PIGS A WASH OF COLOR. THEN USE A PENCIL TO ADD WHISKERS AND MORE FUR TEXTURE, AND TO FURTHER DEFINE THE EARS, EYES, NOSE, AND MOUTH.

A guinea pig's natural habitat is grassy plains, so add some grass to the bottom of your scene!

Try using different colors for the guinea pigs to make each one unique.

SHARK

BASKING SHARK

Draw a large oval for the head, with guidelines for the open mouth and nose. Sketch the body, and smaller ovals and sausage shapes for the fins. Paint gray with white highlights.

These gentle giants swim with their mouths open to filter-feed on plankton.

SHORTFIN MAKO

Pencil a long squashed oval for the body, with small ovals and sausage shapes for the tail and fins. Paint shades of gray with white highlights.

The vertically elongated tail helps propel this shark through the water!

GREAT HAMMERHEAD

Sketch large squashed ovals for the head and body. Add small ovals and sausage shapes for its fins. Paint blue and gray, with white highlights.

Wide-set eyes give this shark a larger visual range.

163

ZEBRA

COMMON PLAINS ZEBRAS, SUCH AS THIS ONE, HAVE TAILS THAT ARE ALMOST HALF A YARD IN LENGTH!

All zebras have different stripe markings, so make yours look just the way you want it to!

1 DRAW A BASIC SHAPE FOR THE ZEBRA. ADD AN OBLONG FOR THE BODY, A SMALL CIRCLE FOR THE HEAD, AND LINES FOR THE LEGS, NECK, AND TAIL.

2 ADD SOME ROUGH LINES TO CONNECT UP ALL THE SHAPES. ADD THE MANE AND TAIL. AT THIS STAGE THE OUTLINE CAN BE QUITE ROUGH.

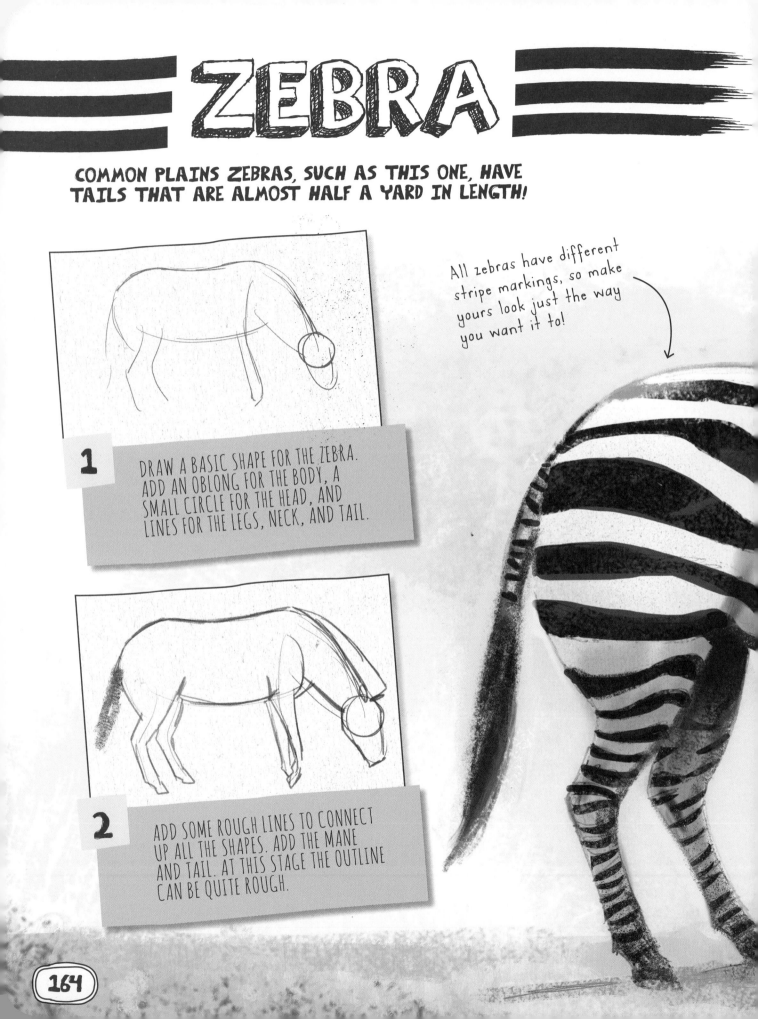

3 ONCE YOU'RE HAPPY WITH THE OVERALL OUTLINE, BEGIN TO ADD SOME DETAILS INCLUDING THE ZEBRA'S EYE, NOSTRIL, MOUTH, AND HOOVES.

4 USE A SOFT PENCIL TO SKETCH IN THE STRIPES ALONG THE ZEBRA'S BODY. KEEP THEM LOOSE AND CHANGE THEM IF THEY DON'T LOOK RIGHT.

5 USE SUBTLE SHADES OF GRAY PENCILS WHEN COLORING THE ZEBRA'S BODY. ADD IN THE FINAL STRIPES ON TOP TO COMPLETE THE DRAWING.

BROWN BEAR

THIS BROWN BEAR IS TRYING TO CATCH SALMON MIDAIR AS THEY JUMP UP THE WATERFALLS!

1

START WITH ONE CIRCLE FOR THE BEAR'S HEAD AND ONE FOR ITS REAR. CONNECT WITH ROUGH LINES. ADD IN FOUR LEG SHAPES, TWO EARS, AND A SHORT SNOUT.

2

CREATE THE OUTLINE OF THE BEAR BY DRAWING ROUGH PENCIL MARKS TO GIVE THE IMPRESSION OF FUZZY FUR. ADD IN ROUGH EYES AND A SMALL NOSE, AND WORK UP THE MOUTH.

3

ERASE THE GUIDELINES AND FILL THE BEAR'S BODY WITH LOTS OF LINES TO SHOW FUR. ADD IN MORE DETAILS, SUCH AS A FEW TEETH AND SHADING UNDERNEATH ITS BODY.

These salmon are moving upstream to lay their eggs. Add a few to your drawing for your hungry bear!

Some brown bears wade into shallow water to catch salmon with their claws. Add another bear on the bank of a river!

4

USE BROWN, ORANGE, AND BLACK CRAYONS TO COLOR THE BEAR'S FUR. USE A BLACK PENCIL TO ADD TEXTURE AND TO FINISH THE FACE, AND PINK FOR THE MOUTH.

PENGUIN

THE EMPEROR PENGUIN IS THE ONLY ANIMAL TO INHABIT THE OPEN ICE OF ANTARCTICA IN WINTER. DRAW YOURS ON AN ICEBERG!

1

START WITH A LONG SQUASHED OVAL FOR THE BODY. ADD IN BASIC SHAPES FOR THE TAIL AND BEAK. DRAW ANOTHER SQUASHED OVAL BELOW FOR THE ICE.

2

USING A SOFT PENCIL, SKETCH AROUND THE GUIDE SHAPES TO FORM THE OUTLINE. ADD A WING, DEFINE THE TAIL AND FEET, AND GIVE THE ICE A JAGGED EDGE.

3

DRAW A LINE TO SHOW THE EDGE OF THE BLACK FEATHER LINE AND A SQUASHED OVAL ON THE SIDE OF THE HEAD. ADD AN EYE, TOES, AND CRACKS TO THE ICE.

4

USE A HARD PENCIL TO ADD DETAILS TO THE HEAD. ADD SHADE TO THE ICE TO SHOW AN UNEVEN SURFACE AND A SHADOW BELOW THE PENGUIN.

168

5

COLOR THE PENGUIN WITH BLACK PENCILS, ADDING
A GRAY WATERCOLOR WASH TO THE CHEST. USE YELLOW
ON THE NECK AND BRIGHT ORANGE ON THE BEAK.

Female penguins lay only
one egg each year. When the
chick hatches, the parents
take turns to feed it.

GRASSHOPPER

THE MOST FREQUENTLY SEEN GRASSHOPPER, THE COMMON FIELD GRASSHOPPER, IS A LARGE INSECT FOUND ACROSS EUROPE, ASIA, AND NORTH AFRICA!

A grasshopper's two back legs are long and powerful for jumping, so don't worry if they look out of proportion compared to the body!

1

BEGIN BY DRAWING A LONG, VERTICAL SAUSAGE SHAPE, THEN ADD A SMALL SQUASHED CIRCLE ON TOP OF IT FOR THE GRASSHOPPER'S HEAD.

2

DRAW TWO LINES—ONE TO DIVIDE THE SAUSAGE SHAPE VERTICALLY AND ONE ANGLED LINE NEAR THE TOP. ROUGH OUT THE POSITIONS OF THE LEGS.

Common field grasshoppers live on a diet of grass, leaves, herbs, shrubs, and bark. Try adding a blade of grass for your grasshopper to munch on!

3

WORK UP THE OUTLINE AND MAKE THE SEGMENTS AND PLATES ON THE BODY BOLDER. DRAW IN AN ALMOND-SHAPED EYE AND A COUPLE OF LONG ANTENNAE ON ITS HEAD.

4

SHADE THE BODY WITH A GREEN PEN. DRAW CROSSHATCHED LINES ON THE WINGS IN A DARKER GREEN OR BROWN. SHADE IN THE EYE A COPPER COLOR.

OCTOPUS

MOST OCTOPUSES CAN CHANGE COLOR AND APPEARANCE TO MIMIC BACKGROUNDS AND SHOW EMOTIONS. THIS ONE IS A GIANT PACIFIC OCTOPUS.

1

DRAW A LARGE OVAL FOR THE HEAD, A SQUASHED OVAL FOR THE BASE OF THE BODY, AND A CIRCULAR EYE.

2

NOW DRAW EIGHT WIGGLY TENTACLES COMING OUT FROM THE BODY. POSITION THEM WHEREVER YOU LIKE!

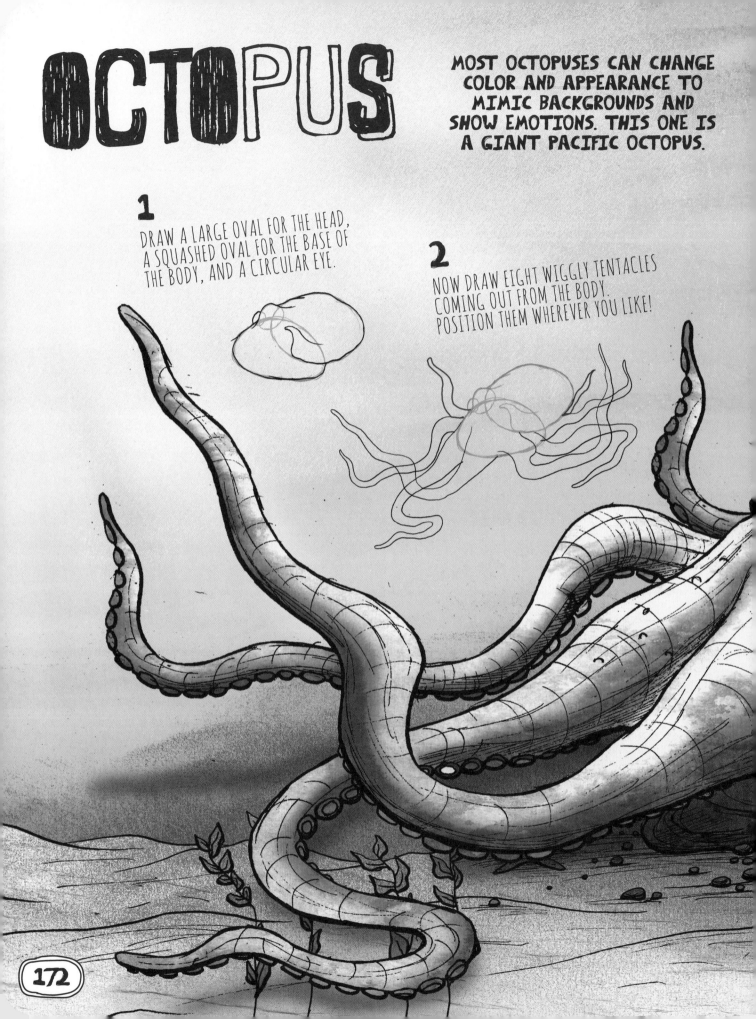

3

DRAW LOTS OF SMALL CIRCLES FOR THE SUCKERS. START AT THE TIP AND WORK YOUR WAY IN TO THE BODY.

4

PAINT THE BODY YELLOW, WITH RED HIGHLIGHTS. ADD MORE RED TO THE SUCKERS, THE EYE, AND PATCHES ON THE SKIN.

SUCKERS ON TENTACLES

For the suckers, start with a simple cylinder and then draw a slightly smaller circle inside to make the rim. Add a very small circle in the center.

AMERICAN LONGHAIR

AMERICAN LONGHAIR CATS ARE LARGE CATS WITH A RECTANGULAR BODY SHAPE AND A LONGHAIRED, FLOWING COAT. THEY COME IN MANY DIFFERENT COLORS!

1

BEGIN BY SKETCHING A ROUGH OUTLINE FOR THE PLAYFUL POSE OF YOUR CAT.

2

ADD IN A FEW DETAILS, SUCH AS THE EARS, EYE, NOSE, MOUTH, AND PAWS.

3

USE A YELLOW CRAYON TO SHADE IN THE EYES AND BODY. THEN USE A BROWN CRAYON TO START ROUGHING OUT FUR TEXTURES AND ADD DEFINITION.

4

USE DIFFERENT SHADES OF BROWN TO BUILD UP THE FUR. LEAVE A LITTLE BIT OF WHITE AND YELLOW UNDERNEATH THE CAT'S FACE AND THE TIP OF ITS PAWS.

GINGER

This fluffy ginger kitten is a bit timid! Use orange, light brown, and white for the fur, pink for the nose, mouth, and ears, and blue for the eyes.

WHITE

To make this white cat stand out, try a bold color for the background. Use beige and gray for shading, and a little pink for its ears and nose.

STRIPY

This cat's fur has stripes of gray, black, and white. Use yellow for the eyes and pink for the tip of the nose.

LEAFCUTTER ANT

1 START OUT BY SKETCHING THREE SQUASHED OVALS. THESE WILL FORM THE HEAD, THORAX, AND ABDOMEN.

2 USING A SOFT PENCIL, CREATE A ROUGH OUTLINE. ADD SIX ROUGH LEG SHAPES, AN EYE, AND MANDIBLES.

4 COLOR YOUR ANT USING BROWN AND RED WATERCOLORS. USE A BLACK PENCIL TO ADD DETAIL.

3 USE A HARD PENCIL TO FINALIZE THE OVERALL OUTLINE. THEN ADD TWO ANTENNAE TO THE HEAD.

Ant colonies use their strength in numbers to work together to protect, build, and supply food for their nests.

Leafcutter ants can carry over 50 times their own body weight! So don't worry if your leaf looks too big compared to the ants.

CRAB

CHRISTMAS ISLAND RED
CRABS ARE LAND CRABS THAT
MASS MIGRATE TO THE
OCEAN EVERY YEAR TO LAY
THEIR EGGS IN THE SEA.

If a Christmas
Island red crab
loses one of its
limbs, it can
grow it back
over time!

1

START WITH TWO CROSSED LINES AS A GUIDE.
DRAW A LARGE OVAL FOR THE BODY, THEN ADD
IN SOME SAUSAGE SHAPES FOR THE LEGS.

2

USING THE GUIDE SHAPES, SKETCH THE ROUGH
OUTLINE OF THE BODY. ADD A SMALL V-SHAPE TO
EACH OF THE TWO FRONT PINCER CLAWS.

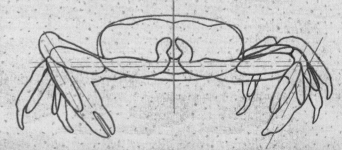

Most of these crabs have a bright red shell, or carapace, but some can be orange or even purple.

3

WITH A HARD PENCIL, ADD IN TWO SMALL EYES AND SKETCH A ROUGH SHAPE FOR THE MOUTH. ADD MORE DETAILS TO THE LEGS.

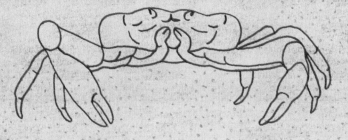

4

BEFORE COLORING, USE A HARD PENCIL TO ADD SOME AREAS OF SHADE TO THE CRAB'S SHELL. COLOR WITH RED, BLACK, AND A LITTLE ORANGE.

MEERKAT

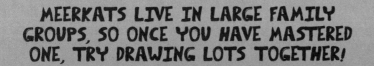

MEERKATS LIVE IN LARGE FAMILY GROUPS, SO ONCE YOU HAVE MASTERED ONE, TRY DRAWING LOTS TOGETHER!

1

DRAW A CIRCLE FOR THE HEAD, OVAL BODY, AND RECTANGULAR-SHAPED ARMS AND LEGS. ADD GUIDELINES FOR THE FACE AND TAIL.

2

USE THE GUIDE SHAPES TO DEFINE THE OUTLINE. ADD IN FACIAL DETAILS USING THE GUIDELINES AND SKETCHY LINES FOR THE FUR.

3

SHADE DARKER AREAS AROUND THE EYES, EARS, AND NOSE. ADD SHADOWS UNDER THE ARMS AND SEPARATE THE PAWS INTO FINGERS.

4

ADD A LITTLE SHINE TO THE
MEERKAT'S NOSE AND DARK
SHADING ON ITS TAIL AND
STOMACH AREA.

5

TO COLOR, KEEP THINGS SIMPLE
WITH BROWN AND GRAY PENCILS ON
THE MEERKAT'S FUR. ADD IN SOME
HIGHLIGHTS WITH A WHITE PENCIL.

Meerkats take it in
turns to stand up
and act as sentries
to warn other
meerkats of danger!

Meerkats have fluffy
fur, so use a soft brush
or pencil to achieve the
right sort of effect!

CHIMPANZEE

CHIMPS ARE MOSTLY FOUND IN RAINFORESTS AND WET SAVANNAS. ALTHOUGH OFTEN ON THE GROUND, THEY SPEND MOST OF THEIR TIME FEEDING AND SLEEPING IN TREES!

1

DRAW A ROUGH EGG SHAPE FOR THE BODY, THEN CIRCLES FOR THE HEAD AND MOUTH. ADD SMALL CIRCLES FOR THE EYES AND AN OVAL EAR.

2

USE THE GUIDE SHAPES TO HELP YOU POSITION THE LEGS AND ARMS, ROUNDING OFF WITH SOCK SHAPES FOR THE HANDS AND FEET.

3

SKETCH IN THE BASIC OUTLINE, WORKING UP THE HANDS AND FEET. BREAK UP THE LINE FOR HAIR AND ADD THE FACIAL FEATURES.

4

NOW ADD DETAIL TO THE FACE, HANDS, FEET, AND BANANA. USE THE HAND AND FEET SHAPES TO HELP POSITION THE FINGERS AND TOES.

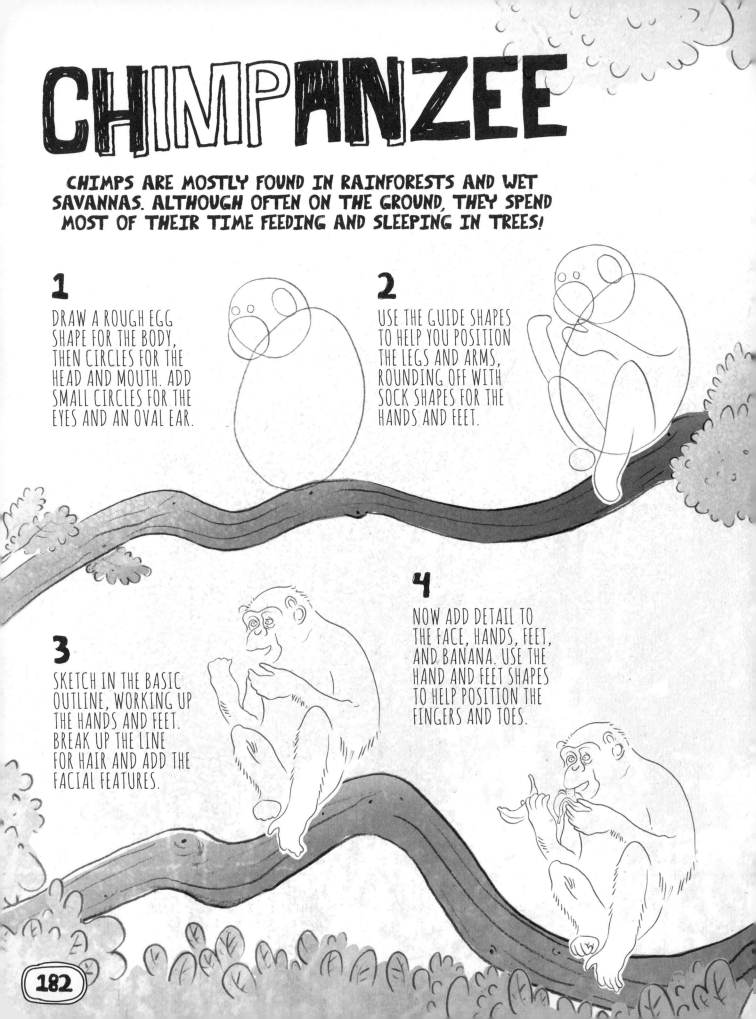

5

TO COLOR, USE A GRAY WATERCOLOR WASH ALL OVER, THEN ADD HAIR STROKES WITH A BLACK PENCIL. USE A PINK PENCIL ON THE FACE, EARS, HANDS, FEET, AND PATCHES OF THE BODY.

Add a lush jungle habitat to your drawing, with a tree branch for the chimpanzee to sit on!

Chimpanzees don't eat bananas as we do—they peel from the non-stem end!

KOMODO DRAGON

1

DRAW A SMALL CIRCLE FOR THE HEAD AND A LARGER CIRCLE FOR THE BODY. ADD ROUGH GUIDELINES FOR THE SPINE, LEGS, AND TAIL.

2

USING A SOFT PENCIL, SKETCH AROUND THE GUIDE SHAPES AND LINES TO CREATE AN OUTLINE OF THE BULKY BODY.

The Komodo dragon's thick, muscular tail is as long as its body!

3

NEXT, USE A HARD PENCIL TO FURTHER REFINE THE OUTLINE. ADD CLAWS ON EACH FOOT, AND EYES, NOSTRILS, AND MOUTH ON THE FACE.

THE KOMODO DRAGON IS THE LARGEST AND MOST POWERFUL LIZARD. ITS NATURAL HABITAT IS THE INDONESIAN ISLAND OF KOMODO, SO DRAW YOURS ON A BEACH!

4

NOW START WORK ON THE TEXTURE OF THE BODY AND SHADE AREAS ON THE LEGS AND TAIL. ADD A LONG TONGUE.

5

COLOR WITH A BROWN AND GRAY WASH. USE A SPLATTER EFFECT WITH A BRUSH FOR THE SCALES OR TRY DABBING THE DRAWING WITH A SPONGE.

DUCK HAWK

DUCK HAWKS ARE THE FASTEST ANIMALS IN THE WORLD. THEY CAN REACH SPEEDS OF UP TO 200 MPH. DRAW YOURS FLYING HIGH!

1

BEGIN WITH A CIRCLE FOR THE BODY. THEN ADD ROUGH SHAPES FOR ITS WINGS AND A CURVED LINE FOR THE HEAD.

2

SKETCH TWO SMALL SAUSAGE SHAPES FOR LEGS. THEN, USING A HARD PENCIL, ADD CLAWS ON EACH OF THE BIRD'S FEET.

3

USING A SOFT PENCIL, ADD FEATHERS TO THE BIRD'S WINGS AND TAIL, MAKING THE TIPS OF THE WINGS DARKER.

4

ADD SOME DETAIL TO THE DUCK HAWK'S FACE WITH TWO EYES AND AN OPEN BEAK WITH NOSTRILS.

5

COLOR THE TOP WITH BROWN AND BLACK PENCILS. FOR THE UNDERSIDE, USE CREAM AND WHITE PENCILS. ADD YELLOW ON THE BEAK AND FEET.

PORCUPINE

PORCUPINES ARE RODENTS WITH SHARP SPINES ON THEIR BODIES. SOME HAVE UP TO 30,000 SPINES, OR QUILLS—SO GRAB A PENCIL AND GO QUILL-CRAZY!

1

LIGHTLY DRAW A LARGE OVAL FOR THE BODY. ADD A SMALL CIRCLE FOR THE HEAD, A SQUASHED OVAL FOR THE PORCUPINE'S TAIL, AND ROUGH LINES FOR THE FOUR LEGS.

2

USING THE GUIDE SHAPES AND LINES, ADD THE FEET, EYE, NOSE, AND EAR, THEN BEGIN ADDING LINES TO SHOW THE DIRECTION OF THE SPINES.

3

SKETCH FUR TEXTURE TO THE OUTLINE OF THE LEGS, CHEST, AND BELLY. DRAW WHISKERS AND CONTINUE TO ADD SPINES UNTIL YOU ARE HAPPY WITH THE SHAPE.

4

COLOR THE BODY WITH BROWN PAINT. USE A BLACK PENCIL TO GO OVER AND BUILD UP THE FUR TEXTURE. SOME OF THE SPINES HAVE CREAM STRIPES ON THEM, SO ADD MARKINGS HERE AND THERE.

Quills are thick hairs coated in a tough material, called keratin, which is the same stuff that makes up our fingernails!

JELLYFISH

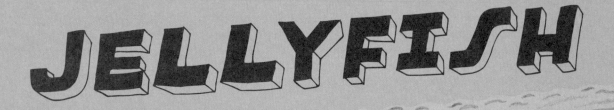

1

START WITH FOUR GUIDELINES. ADD A DOME-SHAPED HEAD ON TOP AND CURVED LINES FOR THE BASIC OUTLINE OF THE JELLYFISH'S TENTACLES.

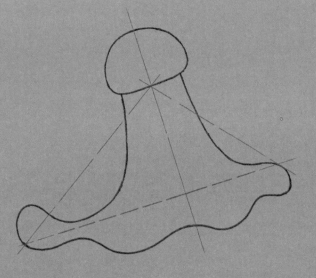

2

USING A SOFT PENCIL, GIVE THE HEAD MORE DEFINITION. THEN TIGHTEN UP THE OVERALL SHAPE OF THE TENTACLES, ADDING A FEW STRAY TENTACLES ON EITHER SIDE.

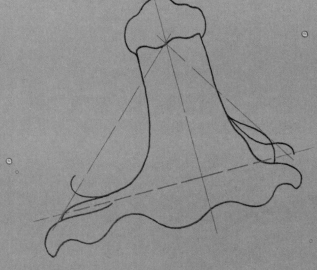

3

ADD MORE DETAIL TO THE DOME, INCLUDING SOME VERTICAL LINES. NOW SKETCH LOTS OF LONG, CURVY LINES FOR THE INDIVIDUAL TENTACLES HANGING BELOW.

The tentacles of a lion's mane jellyfish are grouped into eight clusters. Each cluster can contain up to 100 tentacles!

4

USE A LIGHT PINK WATERCOLOR FOR THE DOME, ADDING ORANGE AND YELLOW HIGHLIGHTS ALONG THE EDGE. COLOR THE TENTACLES WITH YELLOW, ORANGE, AND PINK PENCILS.

WOODLAND BABIES

RACCOON KIT

1

FIRST, DRAW OVALS FOR THE BODY AND HEAD. ADD OVALS FOR EYE PATCHES, SNOUT, AND EARS. ADD SAUSAGE-SHAPED ARMS AND LEGS, AND A U-SHAPED TAIL.

2

USING THE GUIDE SHAPES, SKETCH THE OVERALL OUTLINE. ADD THE RACCOON'S FUR, WITH DARK SHADING AROUND THE EYES AND STRIPES ON THE TAIL.

3

USING A BLACK PENCIL, SHADE AROUND THE EYES, IN THE EARS, AND ON THE TAIL. USE A LITTLE BROWN AND WHITE PAINT TO FINISH THE FUR.

BEAR CUB

1
DRAW A KIDNEY-SHAPED BODY. ADD A CIRCULAR HEAD, TWO EARS, EYES, A DOME-SHAPED SNOUT AND SAUSAGE-SHAPED ARMS, AND LEGS.

2
USING THE GUIDE SHAPES, SKETCH A THICK, SHAGGY COAT. SHADE DARKER AREAS AROUND THE EYES AND INSIDE THE EARS.

3
USE BROWN PAINT FOR THE BEAR'S COAT. GO OVER THE DRAWING WITH A BLACK PEN TO ADD DETAIL TO THE FUR, EYES, AND NOSE.

HEDGEHOG PUP

1
DRAW A SQUASHED OVAL BODY WITH A CURVED LINE FOR THE SNOUT. ADD CIRCLE EYES AND SAUSAGE-SHAPED LEGS.

2
USING THE GUIDE SHAPES, ADD DASHES FOR THE PRICKLES. SHADE DARKER AREAS AROUND THE EYES.

3
USE BROWN, BLACK, AND ORANGE PENCILS FOR THE SPIKES AND A LITTLE PINK FOR THE NOSE AND LEGS.

GREAT WHITE SHARK

1

START WITH TWO OVERLAPPING OVALS—
A SLIGHTLY POINTED ONE FOR THE HEAD
AND A ROUND ONE FOR THE BODY. ADD
A POINTED OVAL FOR THE TAIL.

2

USE A SOFT PENCIL TO DRAW AROUND
THE SHAPES AND FORM THE OVERALL
OUTLINE. ADD LINES FOR THE MOUTH
AND BASIC POINTED FINS.

3

COLOR YOUR SHARK WITH A BLUE AND GRAY WASH. ADD WHITE HIGHLIGHTS AND USE A GRAY PENCIL FOR SHADING AND A FEW SCARS.

Great white sharks have over 100 teeth, but only about 48 are in use. The others are behind, waiting to move forward, replacing the front teeth as they are lost. Try drawing a great white coming out of the water and use a hard pencil to draw lots of sharp teeth in its mouth!

SCORPION

THIS IS AN ASIAN FOREST SCORPION—YOU CAN PROBABLY GUESS WHERE IT COMES FROM ... THE CLUE IS IN THE NAME! SET THE SCENE WITH A TROPICAL RAINFOREST BACKGROUND.

1 START WITH BASIC GUIDELINES FOR THE SCORPION'S BODY, TAIL, LEGS, AND PINCERS.

2 WORK UP THE BODY, TAIL, AND PINCERS AND ADD ROUGH SHAPES FOR ITS EIGHT LEGS.

3 USE A HARD PENCIL TO DEFINE THE OUTLINE. REMOVE GUIDELINES AND SPLIT THE PINCERS.

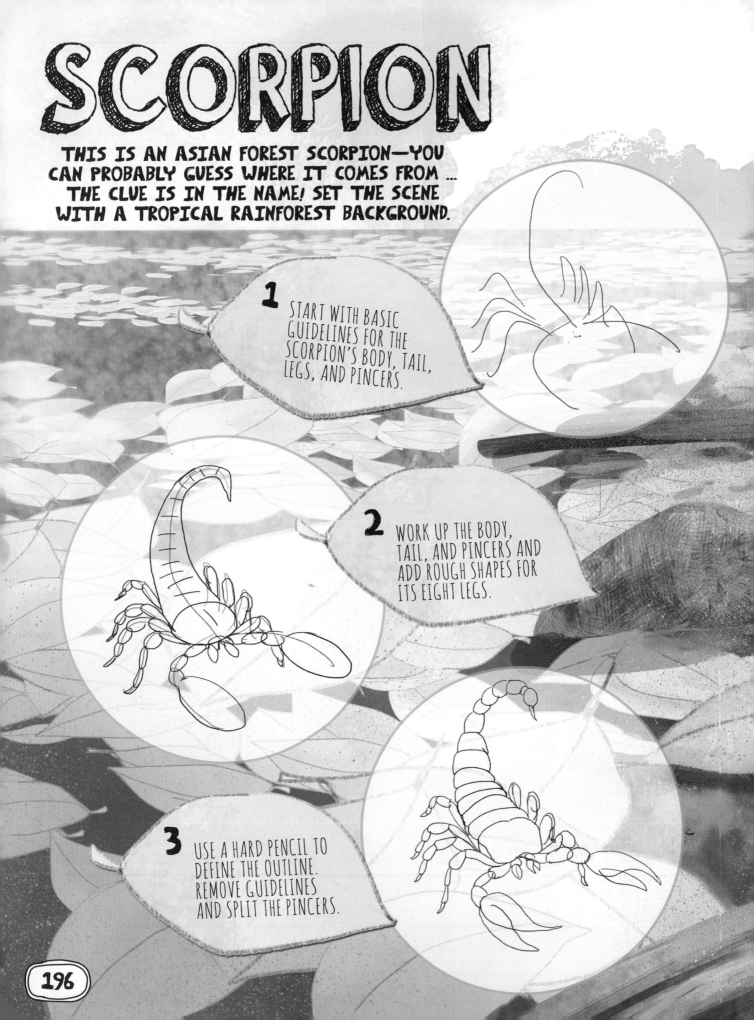

4 ADD MORE DETAILS, SUCH AS HAIRS ON THE SCORPION'S LEGS AND TEXTURES ON ITS SKIN.

5 COLOR USING BROWN, YELLOW, AND BLACK, WITH A HINT OF ORANGE AND RED ON ITS STINGER.

GERMAN SHEPHERD

1 DRAW TWO OVALS—ONE FOR THE BODY AND ONE FOR THE HEAD. DRAW ONE OVAL AND FOUR SAUSAGE SHAPES FOR THE LEGS.

2 ADD TWO TRIANGLE SHAPES FOR THE EARS AND A CIRCLE FOR THE EYE. SKETCH A LONG SAUSAGE SHAPE FOR THE TAIL.

3 USING THE GUIDE SHAPES, CREATE AN OVERALL OUTLINE. THEN DEFINE THE DOG'S SNOUT, EARS, LEGS, AND MOUTH.

4 USING SOFT STROKES, CREATE A FUR EFFECT. PENCIL IN THE NOSE, EYES, AND TONGUE AND SHADE THE INSIDE OF THE EARS.

German shepherds are agile and strong, so they need space to run around freely. Draw yours at a sunny beach, with golden sand and bright blue sky.

5 ADD COLOR USING PAINT OR COLORED PENCILS. USE SOFT STROKES FOR THE LONGHAIRED COAT. USE A SHARP PENCIL TO DEFINE THE EYES AND NOSE.

German shepherds are fast dogs and can run at speeds in excess of 30 mph!

These dogs shed lots of fur and need daily brushing to prevent a buildup of hair.

GIANT TORTOISE

THESE LARGE, SLOW-MOVING REPTILES CAN LIVE FOR UP TO 175 YEARS!

Once colored, add wrinkles, indents, and creases to the shell and skin with a fine pen.

1 BEGIN WITH A BASIC SHELL SHAPE. ADD A ROUGH BODY AND THREE THICK LEGS. DRAW THE NECK AND HEAD IN TWO PARTS, WITH AN OPEN MOUTH.

2 SKETCH A ROUGH SHELL PATTERN, THEN ADD CREASE LINES ON THE SKIN OF THE FEET AND NECK. ADD AN EYE AND NOSTRIL TO THE TORTOISE'S FACE.

3

DRAW SMALL PENTAGON SHAPES WITHIN EACH SHELL SECTION. WORK UP THE SKIN CREASES AND SCALES ON THE FACE AND NECK.

4

USE BROWN AND BLACK PENCILS TO CREATE THE LOOK OF THE SHELL AND SKIN. ADD GREEN AND YELLOW HIGHLIGHTS ALL OVER.

GECKO

THESE LIZARDS ARE FOUND IN WARM CLIMATES AROUND THE WORLD AND COME IN VARIOUS SHAPES AND COLORS. HERE ARE THREE FOR YOU TO DRAW!

NORTHLAND GREEN GECKO

Draw a sloping bean-shaped body with a large oval head and folded legs. Add a long tail, eye, and toes. Connect the shapes and paint green with yellow and gold freckles.

TOKAY GECKO

Draw a bean-shaped body and sausage-shaped tail. Add heart-shaped legs and circular feet. Add the head with an eye and a curved line for its mouth. Paint blue-gray with orange and white spots.

LEOPARD GECKO

Begin by drawing squashed ovals for the head and body. Add a curved tail and small ovals for the legs. Connect the shapes and add an eye and mouth. Paint yellow and orange, with black spots.

POLAR BEAR

1

START WITH TWO OVERLAPPING CIRCLES FOR THE MAIN SECTIONS OF THE POLAR BEAR'S BODY. ADD A CIRCLE FOR THE HEAD.

2

NOW DRAW IN THE FOUR LEGS, BREAKING EACH DOWN INTO TWO PARTS—A SQUASHED OVAL AND SQUASHED SAUSAGE SHAPES.

3

USE A SOFT PENCIL TO SKETCH AROUND THE SHAPES AND FORM THE OUTLINE. ADD DETAILS INCLUDING TOES ON EACH FOOT, AND EARS.

4

ADD MORE DETAILS TO YOUR DRAWING BY PENCILING IN THE INNER PART OF THE EAR, TWO EYES, A NOSE, MOUTH, AND SHARP CLAWS.

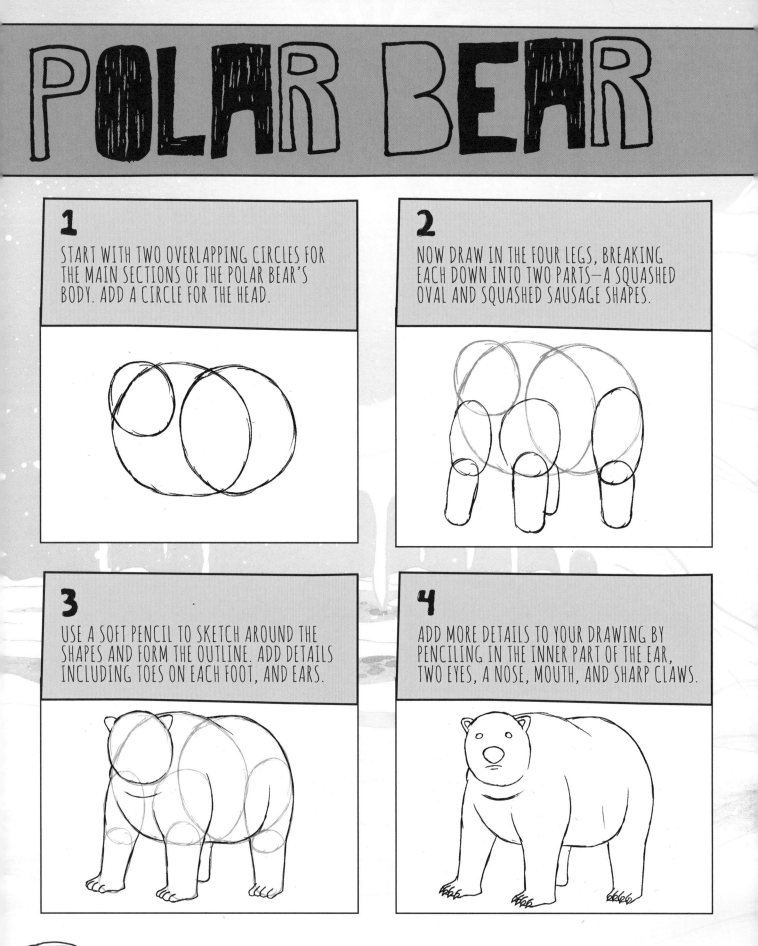

ALTHOUGH POLAR BEARS ARE BORN ON LAND, THEY SPEND MOST OF THEIR TIME IN THE SEA, HUNTING SEALS.

5

COLOR WHITE, BUT USE A LIGHT YELLOW WATERCOLOR WASH ON SOME OF THE FUR. USE A BROWN PENCIL TO ADD FUR DETAIL.

Polar bears have black skin and transparent, hollow hairs that reflect light, making them look white.

CUB

1
DRAW SQUASHED OVALS FOR THE NECK, BODY, LEGS, AND FEET. ADD A CIRCULAR HEAD.

2
SKETCH THE OUTLINE AND BREAK UP THE LINE TO SHOW SOFT FUR. ADD EARS, EYES, NOSE, AND A MOUTH.

3
AS WITH THE ADULT, COLOR WHITE WITH A LIGHT YELLOW WASH. ADD HIGHLIGHTS WITH A BROWN PENCIL.

GAZELLE

LEARN TO DRAW A DORCAS GAZELLE, ALSO KNOWN AS THE ARIEL GAZELLE!

1

START BY DRAWING CIRCLES, OVALS, AND SAUSAGE SHAPES FOR THE HEAD, NECK, BODY, LEGS, EARS, AND HORNS.

2

USE A SOFT PENCIL TO DRAW ALL AROUND THE SHAPES TO DEFINE CLEARLY THE BASIC OUTLINE OF THE GAZELLE.

3

NOW START TO ADD SOME DETAIL TO THE GAZELLE'S FACE AND BODY. ADD IN TWO EYES, AS WELL AS A SMALL NOSE AND MOUTH.

4

SKETCH MORE DETAIL ON THE BODY, HOOVES, AND TAIL. USE THE SOFT PENCIL AGAIN TO SOFTEN UP ANY HARD LINES ON THE BODY.

A female gazelle's horns are much smaller and straighter than those of the males.

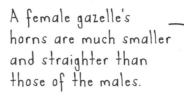

A male gazelle's horns are lyre-shaped and up to 16 in long. Some have horns that grow down instead of up.

5

COLOR YOUR GAZELLE WITH A SELECTION OF BROWNS AND ORANGES. ADD SOME FINAL TOUCHES TO THE FACE, TAIL, AND HOOVES WITH A SHARP BLACK PENCIL.

GIRAFFE

EACH SPECIES OF GIRAFFE HAS A CHARACTERISTIC COLOR AND PATTERN. THIS ONE IS A WEST AFRICAN GIRAFFE, WHICH HAS LIGHT-COLORED SPOTS.

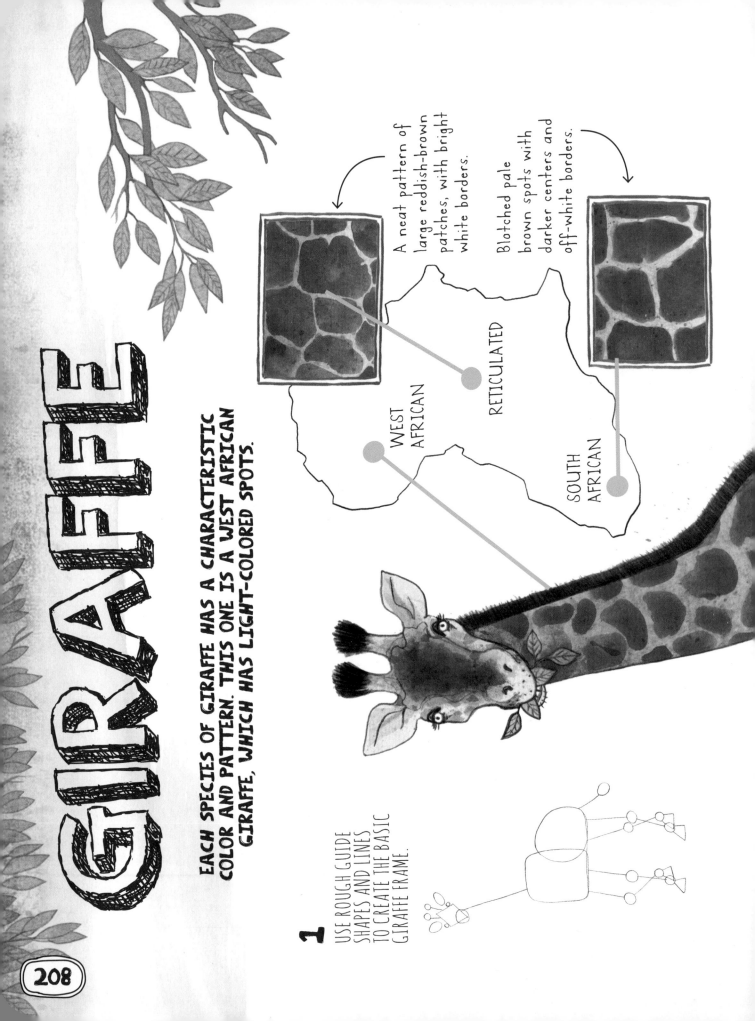

A neat pattern of large reddish-brown patches, with bright white borders.

Blotched pale brown spots with darker centers and off-white borders.

WEST AFRICAN

RETICULATED

SOUTH AFRICAN

1

USE ROUGH GUIDE SHAPES AND LINES TO CREATE THE BASIC GIRAFFE FRAME.

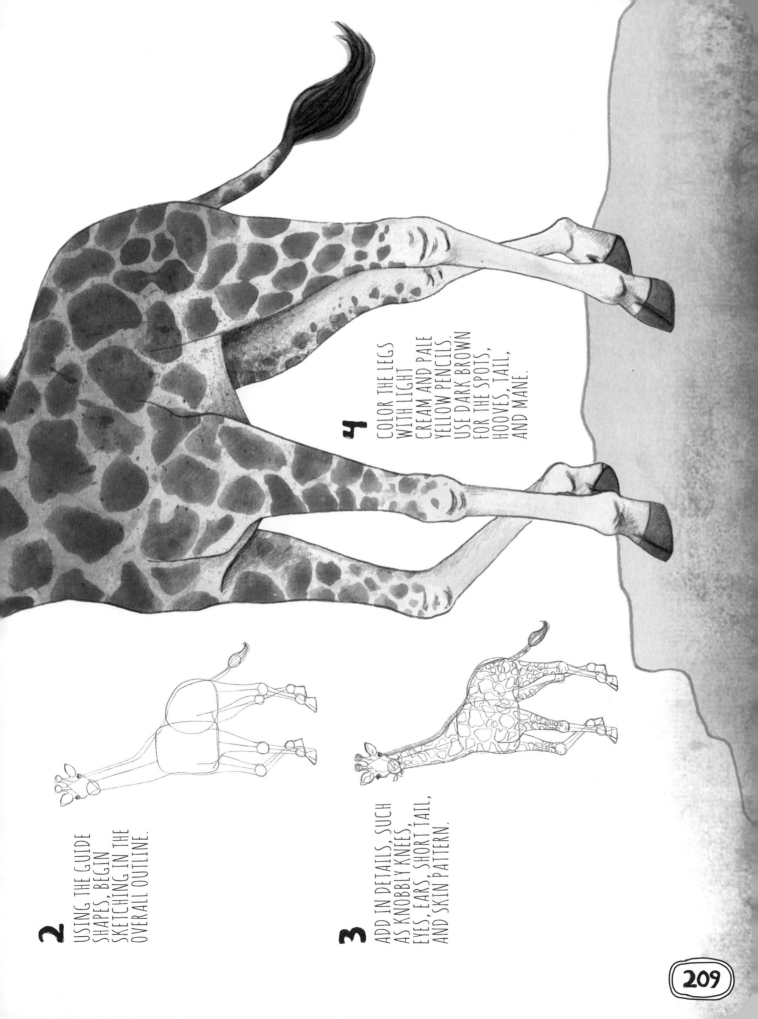

4

COLOR THE LEGS WITH LIGHT CREAM AND PALE YELLOW PENCILS. USE DARK BROWN FOR THE SPOTS, HOOVES, TAIL, AND MANE.

2

USING THE GUIDE SHAPES, BEGIN SKETCHING IN THE OVERALL OUTLINE.

3

ADD IN DETAILS, SUCH AS KNOBBLY KNEES, EYES, EARS, SHORT TAIL, AND SKIN PATTERN.

DINGO

1

DRAW CIRCLES FOR THE BODY AND HEAD. ADD TWO TRIANGLE EARS AND THREE SAUSAGE-SHAPED LEGS.

2

SKETCH IN THE OUTLINE. ADD EYES, A NOSE, AND FACIAL MARKINGS. DRAW VERTICAL LINES ON THE FEET FOR TOES.

1

FOR THE ADULT DINGO, DRAW A BEAN SHAPE FOR THE BODY, WITH OVALS FOR THE HEAD AND HIPS. ADD ROUGH LEGS AND A TAIL.

2

WORK UP THE OUTLINE OF THE DINGO AND ADD BASIC DETAILS TO THE EARS, FACE, AND PAWS. USE A SOFT PENCIL TO CREATE FUR TEXTURE.

Draw large areas of arid desert and open bush to set the scene!

A dingo has a long, tapered muzzle and its ears are large and pointed!

COLOR!

COLOR WITH SOFT BROWN, ORANGE AND YELLOW CRAYONS. USE A BLACK PENCIL TO FINISH THE EYES, NOSE, AND MOUTH.

SWAN

THIS BEWICK'S SWAN IS NAMED AFTER THOMAS BEWICK, WHO ILLUSTRATED BIRDS AND ANIMALS.

1 DRAW OVALS FOR THE SWAN'S BODY AND TAIL, A CIRCLE FOR THE HEAD, AND A CURVED LINE FOR THE NECK. ADD A TRIANGLE FOR THE BEAK.

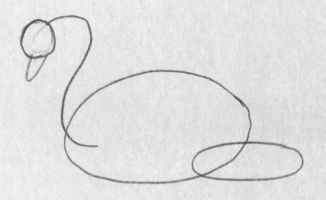

2 SKETCH AROUND THE SHAPES TO FORM THE OUTLINE OF THE SWAN, DEFINING THE SHAPE OF THE HEAD, NECK, BEAK, AND WING.

Swan couples build strong bonds and often stay together for life. Once you've drawn one swan, try drawing its mirror image.

3 ADD MORE DETAIL TO THE FEATHERS, BEAK, AND EYES. USE A HARD PENCIL TO GET PLENTY OF LINE DEFINITION.

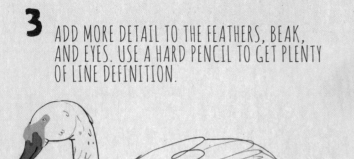

Swans are among the largest flying birds. They can be up to 5 ft in length!

4 CREATE A FEATHERY EFFECT WITH SOFT PENCIL STROKES. USE A SHARP BLACK PENCIL TO ADD THE EYES AND NOSE. USE BRIGHT YELLOW FOR ITS BEAK.

BULLDOG

1 START WITH TWO CIRCLES AS A GUIDE FOR THE BODY, A CIRCLE AS A GUIDE FOR THE HEAD, LARGE OVALS FOR THE LEGS, AND SMALL OVALS FOR THE EARS, TAIL, AND FEET.

2 USING THE GUIDE SHAPES, SKETCH A ROUGH OUTLINE FOR THE BULLDOG. THEN DRAW A CROSS FOR THE FACE—A CURVED VERTICAL LINE AND A HORIZONTAL LINE FOR THE EYES.

3 USING THE GUIDELINES, DRAW BASIC EYES, NOSE, MOUTH, BONE, TONGUE, AND CHIN. DEFINE THE OUTLINE OF THE BULLDOG, INCLUDING THE EARS, TAIL, LEGS, AND FEET.

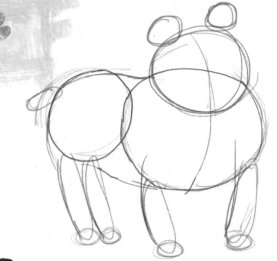

Bulldogs have folds of skin on the brow, wide-set eyes, folds above the nose, drooping lips, and hanging skin under the chin.

4 ADD THE FINAL DETAILS TO YOUR DRAWING BEFORE THE COLORING STAGE, INCLUDING THE COLLAR AND ROLLS OF SKIN. THEN FURTHER DEFINE THE HEAVY FEET AND MUSCULAR BODY.

Try adding some mud splats and paw-prints to your drawing!

5 USE DIFFERENT SHADES OF BROWN PAINT TO COLOR. ADD BLACK FOR THE NOSE AND ANY DARKER AREAS. COLOR THE TONGUE WITH A LITTLE PINK AND SHADE THE BONE WITH YELLOW AND WHITE.

AxOLOTL

THIS ODD-LOOKING CREATURE IS KNOWN AS A WALKING FISH—BUT IT IS NOT A FISH, IT IS AN AMPHIBIAN! LEARN TO DRAW THIS UNIQUE ANIMAL.

1

DRAW A SQUASHED OVAL HEAD, SMALL EYES, AND A CURVED MOUTH. SKETCH A SEMICIRCLE FOR THE BODY AND ADD ARMS, FINGERS, AND GILL STALKS.

The feathery stalks at the back of the axolotl's head are its external gills!

2

NEXT, ADD MORE SHAPE TO THE HEAD. USING THE EDGE OF YOUR PENCIL, CREATE QUICK FLICKS FOR THE FEATHERY EFFECT ON THE GILL STALKS.

3

COLOR WITH A PINK WATERCOLOR WASH, THEN USE PINK FELT-TIP PENS TO SHADE THE GILL STALKS AND ADD SHADOWS. COLOR THE EYES BLUE.

1

FOR THIS POSE, DRAW A LONG SQUASHED OVAL FOR THE BODY. ADD A RIDGE ON ITS BACK, THREE LEGS, TOES, GILL STALKS, AND AN EYE.

2

USING THE GUIDE SHAPES, SKETCH THE OVERALL OUTLINE. ADD IN THE GILL STALKS AROUND THE HEAD, THEN A MOUTH AND SMALL TOES.

3

START WITH A PALE PINK WATERCOLOR BASE, THEN USE A PINK FELT-TIP PEN FOR THE GILL STALKS. ADD ORANGE HIGHLIGHTS OVER THE BODY.

Axolotls have almost translucent skin, so keep your watercolor wash light!

CROCODILE

THESE BRAVE EGYPTIAN PLOVERS ARE PICKING OUT SMALL BITS OF FOOD FROM THIS NILE CROCODILE'S MOUTH. THE BIRDS GET FED AND THE CROCODILE GETS ITS TEETH CLEANED!

1

START WITH A V-SHAPED LINE, DIVIDED INTO THREE SECTIONS. THEN ADD AN OVAL FOR THE BODY AND A CURVED LINE FOR THE MOUTH.

4

SKETCH SHADOWS INSIDE THE MOUTH. ADD A VERTICAL SLIT PUPIL, AND WING AND EYE DETAILS TO THE BIRDS.

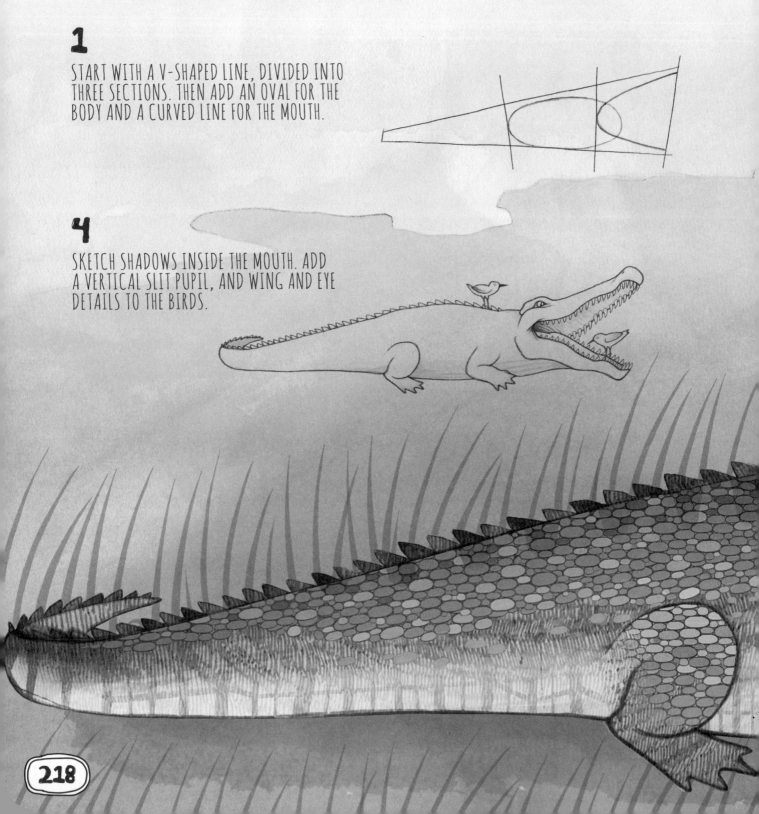

2

ADD TWO HEART-SHAPED LEGS AND WORK UP
THE BASIC SHAPE OF THE MOUTH. SKETCH OVALS
TO SHOW WHERE THE BIRDS WILL PERCH.

3

JOIN THE SHAPES INTO THE OUTLINE. ADD
DETAILS, INCLUDING WEBBED FEET, A SPIKY
BACK, AND SHARP TEETH. SKETCH THE BIRDS.

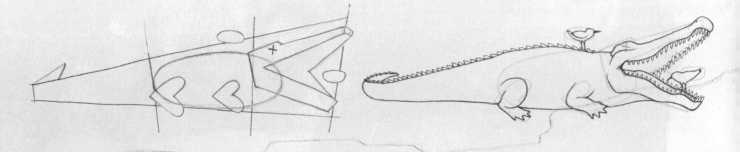

A crocodile's nostrils, eyes,
and ears are on the top of
its head so that its body can
stay hidden underwater!

5

COLOR WITH BROWNS AND GREENS. ADD A BIT
OF PINK INSIDE THE MOUTH AND USE GREEN
AND BROWN PENCILS FOR SCALE DETAIL.

INDEx

ABOUT THE ARTISTS

TALENTED ARTISTS FROM AROUND THE WORLD HAVE CONTRIBUTED THEIR SKILLS AND ILLUSTRATIONS TO THIS BOOK!

SOPHIE BURROWS draws all sorts of things for children's books and greeting cards, and especially loves drawing silly animals and cute kids. Her favorite food is pizza and her favorite animals are kittens!

ADAM FISHER has always been fascinated by wildlife. He began drawing animals at a young age and still keeps a book of patterns and shapes found in nature. He uses the textures of fur, feathers, and scales in his work.

JESSICA KNIGHT enjoys working with mixed media and especially loves drawing tigers and anything to do with the sea. When not doodling, daydreaming, or dancing around her studio, she likes walking by the river with Chekhov, her imaginary pet dachshund.

JUN-GU NOH lives and works in Seoul, South Korea. After graduating from Hongik University, he spent one year in England studying Illustration at Kingston University. Since his work appeared on window and package design in 2005, he has been working as an illustrator mainly for printed media.

STEVE STONE lives in Derbyshire, England, with his wife and Vincent, a very cheeky ginger cat. He adores animals—they inspire most of his picture books and paintings.

SI CLARK started drawing at a very early age and has pretty much been illustrating and animating every day since then. Si is obsessed with drawing trees and cities, as well as finding strange textures to scan into his drawings!

AVA MUSE loves to illustrate animals and nature—especially insects, birds, and river wildlife. She is passionate about animal welfare and conservation, and tries to promote this within her work.

STEVE HORROCKS lives in California with his wife, where he works at a major feature animation studio and continues to pursue his passion for creating art at a personal level, too.

You know the materials. You know the techniques.
You've mastered scales, feathers, and prints!
You can draw life in the sea and life in the air,
slimy amphibians, hairy mammals, and creepy crawlies!

So go and sketch, practice,
doodle, and DRAW ANIMALS!